Japanese Foreign Aid

Sukehiro Hasegawa

The Praeger Special Studies program—
utilizing the most modern and efficient book
production techniques and. a selective
worldwide distribution network—makes
available to the academic, government, and
business communities significant, timely
research in U.S. and international economic, social, and political development.

Japanese Foreign Aid
Policy and Practice

PRAEGER SPECIAL STUDIES IN INTERNATIONAL POLITICS AND GOVERNMENT

Praeger Publishers   New York   Washington   London

Library of Congress Cataloging in Publication Data

Hasegawa, Sukehiro.
    Japanese foreign aid.

    (Praeger special studies in international politics and government)
    Bibliography: p.
    1. Economic assistance, Japanese.   2. Technical assistance, Japanese.   I. Title.
HC462.9.H235   338.91'52   74-14813
ISBN 0-275-05510-8

PRAEGER PUBLISHERS
111 Fourth Avenue, New York, N.Y. 10003, U.S.A.

Published in the United States of America in 1975
by Praeger Publishers, Inc.

Printed in the United States of America

This book attempts to explain about the role of Japanese foreign aid in the attainment of Japan's own evolving national goals. It examines the aid policy and practice, taking into consideration Japanese understanding of social nexus and their perception of national and international developments.

Over the 20-year period from 1953 to 1973 Japanese foreign aid was extended with primary objective of augmenting Japan's kokueki (the national interest) and attaining ultimately two basic national goals: her own national development and international ascendancy. As the nature of the basic goals changed over the years, so did the priorities of immediate aid objectives. During the first ten years Japanese aid was extended for immediate commercial objectives and domestic material prosperity. During the following ten years it was increasingly directed at the improvement of the societal welfare of Japan as a whole and the pursuit of her leadership role in the Asian region as well as the establishment of her "proper" place in the global community for their sense of otsukiai (associational obligation). In Chapter 1, the relationship between the national goals and the aid objectives are studied in detail.

In Chapter 2, the official version of Japan's aid policy is reviewed. The government of Japan claimed that Japan was providing aid to less-developed countries because international peace and a viable world economy, essential for Japan's own security and prosperity, depended on the improvement of living conditions in the less-developed countries, and it was a responsibility of Japan as a member of kokusai shakai (the international community). The government, furthermore, claimed that the volume of Japanese aid had substantially increased and its terms had been noticeably improved.

In Chapter 3 and 5, the composition, magnitudes and distribution of aid resources are analyzed and evaluated in detail. The overall volume of so-called aid resources increased steadily during the first ten years and rapidly since then. This increase, however, resulted more from a large expansion of the private and "other official" flows than from an increase in official development assistance, which alone should be considered as constituting genuine aid. According to an economic valuation analysis the terms of Japanese aid loans eased, as evidenced in the marked increase in their weighted average grant cost-element, from 17.5 percent in 1958 to 43.0 percent in 1973.

During the 1950s most of Japanese aid resources were delivered as part of the baisho (reparations). As ascertained in Chapter 4, its primary objective was political, i.e. recovery of Japanese sovereignty over her territories held by the Allied Powers. In the 1960s the

v

government of Japan set forth a scheme called kaibatsu yunyu (development-cum-import) aimed at encouraging production of raw materials ss and primary products and reducing trade imbalances in favor of Japan. Under this scheme, however, Japanese capital and technology ended up more in countries with vital energy and mineral resources than in countries without any significant resources. In Chapter 6, the scheme is critically examined in terms of its proclaimed objective and actual outcome.

Japan's use of her aid as a means to attain international ascendancy was successful in the Asian region but only marginal in the global context. While Japan sought and secured successfully a leadership position in Asia through active participation in and promotion of ECAFE, Colombo Plan, the Mekong Project, the Asian Development Bank and Ministerial Conference for Economic Development of Southeast Asia, she made little serious attempt to play an influential role in such global cooperative agencies as the World Bank and the UNDP. Globally Japan adopted the attitude of otsukiai. Chapter 7 elaborates on the outcome of Japanese policy toward multilateral aid agencies and program.

Chapters 8 and 9 ascertain how Japanese aid policy is formulated and implemented and the major problems of Japanese technical assistance program.

Three principal ministries, Gaimusho (the Ministry of Foreign Affairs), Tsusansho (the Ministry of International Trade and Industry), and Okurasho (the Ministry of Finance) competed in determination of Japanese aid policies while three agencies, Export-Import Bank, OECF, and OTCA emerged as major implementing agencies. Attempts were made without much success to coordinate formulation and implementation of aid policies and measures. Finally, despite Japan's claim that she can be most effective in the transfer of modern technical know-how to less-developed countries, Japanese technical assistance had limited success for political, socio-cultural and linguistic factors.

The author wishes to express his appreciation to Professors Stanley Spector, John W. Bennett, Nicholas Demerath, Charles L. Leven, and Robert Morgan of Washington University who advised him when the original version of this book was drafted as his doctoral dissertation. He is also indebted to his colleagues in Japanese government agencies and the United Nations Development Programme who offered him constructive criticism. However, the views expressed are those of the author and do not necessarily reflect on those of his advisers, colleagues and UNDP, his present employer. Any errors committed are of course the author's responsibility.

CONTENTS

LIST OF TABLES

LIST OF FIGURES

GLOSSARY

AsDB	Asian Development Bank.
baisho	reparations.
CABEI	Central American Bank for Economic Integration.
DAC	Development Assistance Committee of the OECD. Its members in 1973 were Australia, Austria, Belgium, Canada, Denmark, France, the Federal Republic of Germany, Italy, Japan, the Netherlands, New Zealand, Norway, Portugal, Sweden, Switzerland, the United Kingdom, the United States, and the Commission of the European Economic Community.
DAG	Development Assistance Group of the OEEC, predecessor of DAC.
Daitowa kyoeiken	"Greater East Asia Co-prosperity Sphere."
ECAFE	Economic Commission for Asia and the Far East.
ECLA	Economic Commission for Latin America.
ECOSOC	Economic and Social Council of the United Nations.
EPTA	Expanded Programme of Technical Assistance of the United Nations.
Eximbank of Japan	Export-Import Bank of Japan.
Fiscal year	Japanese fiscal year runs from April 1 to March 31.
Fukoku kyohei	"Enrichment of Japan and strengthening of her forces."
Gaimusho	The Ministry of Foreign Affairs of Japan.
GV	Grant-value.
GE	Grant-element.
Happo-yabure	"Defenseless on all sides."
IBRD	International Bank for Reconstruction and Development, the official name of the World Bank.
IDA	International Development Corporation, an affiliate of the IBRD.
IDA	Inter-American Development Bank.
IMF	Internationals Monetary Fund.

Khmer Republic	Cambodia until November 1970.
Kaihatsu yunyu	"Development-cum-import."
kokueki	"The national interest of Japan."
Kokusai shakai	"The international community."
Kokutai	"The national essence or policy of Japan."
ODA	Official development assistance.
OECD	Organisation for Economic Co-operation and Development, successor of the OEEC.
OECF	Overseas Economic Cooperation Fund of Japan.
OEEC	Organization for European Economic Co-operation.
OPEC	Organization of Petroleum Exporting Countries.
Okurasho	The Ministry of Finance of Japan.
OTCA	Overseas Technical Cooperation Agency of Japan.
Otsukiai	"associational obligation."
Rekkyo koku	"leading powers."
Senshinkoku	"advanced countries."
Sekai kyodotai	"The world community."
Special Fund (UN)	A separate fund of the United Nations established by General Assembly resolution 1240 (XIII) in October 1958; predecessor of UNDP.
Tsusansho	The Ministry of International Trade and Industry (MITI) of Japan.
UNCDF	United Nations Capital Development Fund established by the General Assembly resolution 2186 (XXI) in December 1966.
UNDP	United Nations Development Programme

In this book Mr. Hasegawa ascertains evolutionary changes taking place in the objectives and nature of Japanese foreign aid. He analyzes well how Japanese aid is used to attain the ultimate national goals of Japan: her own national development and international ascendency.

I do not necessarily agree with every assertion made by the author in this book. But, it is a book which I recommend to those who wish to gain an overall understanding of Japanese aid in a fairly systematic manner.

Saburo Okita
President
Overseas Economic Co-operation Fund

Japanese
Foreign Aid

1

CONTEMPORARY AND HISTORICAL NATIONAL EVOLUTIONALIST VIEWS

Over the last quarter of a century the flow of foreign aid into less-developed countries has become one of the most widely discussed subjects among observers of international relations and development. Most of these observers agree on the existence of multiple foreign aid objectives; they differ, however, on the importance of any particular objective or motive in the formulation and implementation of aid policies. The objectives and motives they have most frequently cited for foreign aid are the maintenance of national security, the maintenance or transformation of political and social systems, the gaining of presence and recognition in recipient countries, the attainment of international leadership and influence, the pursuing of economic interests, the pursuing of moral and humanitarian considerations, and the achievement of international solidarity and world communalism. [1]

The national security objective is generally considered to be the most prominent motivating factor in foreign aid. The supplying country in this case extends military and economic aid to friendly countries to increase their security against possible external enemies. Both the United States and the Soviet Union are known to have provided a significant amount of aid for this purpose during the postwar era of East-West confrontation (from 1945 to 1972). In fact, in his study of American and Soviet aid programs, Robert S. Walters noted that security considerations have played the major role among the motivations underlying American and Soviet aid programs. [2] Foreign aid is also provided to support governments in certain less-developed countries not only against external threats, but also internal threats, to their security; in so doing the contributing country hopes to maintain a favorable political, economic, and social system in a recipient country. Both American aid to Greece and Soviet aid to Cuba are examples of this type of assistance. Similarly, an aid-supplying country may hope to bring about a transformation of the existing system in a recipient nation to one desired by the supplier.

1

The supplying country may also be interested merely in asserting her presence in recipient countries, and in maintaining a high level of recognition by host governments. For example the United Kingdom and France have had their nationals remain in their former colonial territories long after these territories achieved political independence. Chinese aid to certain East African countries in recent years can also be classified under this type of aid.

Another aid objective is to establish and sustain an influential position in the arena of international parliamentary diplomacy. With an increasing number of regional and global government conferences being held under the auspices of the United Nations, for example, some of the aid-supplying nations are inclined to use their assistance as a tool to influence the voting of their recipient countries. Until the admission of the People's Republic of China to the United Nations in 1971, the U.S. delegates warned some of the recipients of American aid of the possibility of congressional actions against the continuance of aid flows to these recipient nations were they to vote against a position taken by the United States.

Apart from these primarily political motives, the donor country extends aid to serve her own economic interests, and particularly to increase her exports, secure adequate supplies of raw materials, and create a favorable climate for private investments in the recipient countries. The economic motive has in fact been given primary importance in many aid programs.

Moral and humanitarian considerations also constitute a powerful motivating factor. This factor was strongly endorsed by the Pearson Commission in 1969. In response to the contention that the rich countries could not help other nations when they are confronted with their own social and economic problems, the commission appealed directly to moral principles. "The simplest answer to the question is the moral one: that it is only right for those who have to share with those who have not."[3] The Pearsonian rationale advocated that the ultimate objective of development assistance was the establishment of a durable working relationship between the developed and less-developed countries in a new and interdependent world community.

Similar in nature, but different in significance, is the objective of Scandinavian aid programs, which is to strengthen international solidarity and to realize equitable sharing of international wealth. The ultimate goal of this program is the creation of a global welfare state.[4] As Gunnar Myrdal noted, assistance to less-developed countries is in this regard "a collective responsibility for the developed countries, the burden of which should be shared in an agreed fair way, amounting to an approach of a system of international taxation."[5] Such a goal, however, has yet to be firmly supported by a majority of aid suppliers.

CONTEMPORARY VIEWS ON JAPANESE FOREIGN AID OBJECTIVES

In the case of Japanese foreign aid, both foreign and Japanese observers agree on the prominence of the economic motive. Their views and thoughts on Japan's aid program can be divided into five groups that characterize Japanese aid as a manifestation of (1) Japanese economic nationalism, (2) nonideological economic expansionism, (3) ideological expansionism, (4) self-preservationism, and (5) world communalism. The first view of Japanese aid—as a reflection of economic nationalism—is advocated by those observers who regard economic nationalism as the primary aid force and the nation-state as playing the basic role in the international system. Foreign observers tend to support the theory of nonideological economic expansionism, while Marxist scholars in Japan and abroad assert the theory of ideological expansionism. The theory of self-preservationism is presented by those who see an economic limit within which Japan can support her own population. The theory of world communalism is put forward by those who see the importance of foreign aid in the formation of sekai kyodotai, or a world community, in a manner similar to the programs advocated by Pearson and Myrdal.

The economic nationalism view of foreign aid regards on one hand the economic nationalism of Japan and the advanced countries of Europe and North America, which it sees as the most powerful aid force in the postwar era, and on the other hand the economic nationalism of the newly independent nations of Asia, Africa, and Latin America. According to this view the economic nationalism of the advanced countries is manifested in their desire to bring about sustained economic growth and welfare, whereas the economic nationalism of the newly developing nations is reflected in their desire to establish viable national economies and to ultimately realize their economic independence. The key proponent of this view in Japan has been Yoichi Itagaki, who believes the developed countries must learn to understand and appreciate the economic nationalism of the developing nations. Aid and economic cooperation, in Itagaki's view, should be undertaken in the spirit of partnership, with the aim being to assist in the formation and development of indigenous integrated national economies. [6]

The advocates of the nonideological economic expansionist view of foreign aid believe Japanese aid is aimed solely at serving the interest of the expanding Japanese economy. This view maintains that, as Japan pursues her economic well-being, she uses her aid only to encourage a system of interchange between Japan and other countries, and that Japan does not hold a deep rationale or ideology regarding foreign aid, but merely pursues her course of economic expansion and efficiency. John White, for example, concluded in the early 1960s that Japan had neither profound sympathy toward less-developed countries nor a sense of international responsibility. According to

White, Japanese foreign aid during the 1960s had three main objectives—the promotion of Japanese export, the maintenance of Japanese
good faith with the advanced Western countries, and the establishment
of an international framework in which Japan could later exert her influence. "Of these, " White noted, "promotion of exports is by far the
most important. The Government has shown some ingenuity in recon-
ciling all three objectives within a single policy, but in those areas
where a conflict of interest does arise it is almost always the exporters
who come out on top. "[7] White noted further that "what is missing from
Japanese motivations is the concept, which is present to some extent
in the motives of most other donor countries, of an aid policy as a
contribution to an international programme of political and economic
growth. "[8]

Goran Ohlin supported White's view a few years later, noting
that Japanese aid policy largely served the purpose of her own economic
growth and expansion. This theory of nonideological expansionism was
also advanced by Leon Hollerman, who pointed out that one of the basic
objectives of Japanese aid was to promote exports of heavy industrial
and chemical products. [9] And in 1972 Samuel P. Huntington gave further
emphasis to this theory in noting that Japan's expanding aid was also
directed at extending Japanese commerce and investments in Asia. [10]
Also in 1972, U. S. government researchers elaborated the notion of
economic motives by pointing out Japan's usage of aid for the purpose
of obtaining food and other raw materials. "Japan's foreign aid or
economic cooperation policy, " these researchers noted, "is closely
tied to its commercial policies of maximizing exports of industrial
products and diversifying import sources of food and industrial raw
materials. "[11]

The ideological expansionist view of Japanese aid has been put
forth by those who see a Japanese design or scheme to bring neighboring countries of Asia under her control; the most outspoken advocates of this view have been Marxist scholars in Japan and abroad.
Among these scholars are Japanese Marxist economist Kazuji Nagasu
and British observers John Halliday and Gavan McCormack, who
indicated it is inevitable that the Japanese will extend their sphere
of domination so long as their capitalist economy continues to expand.
Even such moderates as Tadashi Kawata noted that Japanese foreign
aid is used to facilitate katagawari, a process by which Japan shoul-
ders the burden of maintaining existing international structures.

Nagasu observed that aid and economic cooperation are extended
by Japan to serve its own domestic prosperity, and not at all for mere
humanitarian motives. First, according to Nagasu, the volume of
Japanese aid has been expanding parallel to the growth of the Japanese
economy (it became the second largest aid program among the world's
leading donors in the 1970s). Second, the Japanese aid program has
been transformed from one of compensating for the "wrong doings"
done by the Japanese during World War II, Nagasu noted, to one in

which the Japanese manifested an attitude called otsukiai, as a
member of the Organisation for Economic Cooperation and Development (OECD), and, finally, to one where the emphasis has been on
spontaneous and active economic expansion and aggrandizement.
Otsukiai is defined as an attitude or action taken for the sake of
preserving Japanese associations, friendships, and alliances. Third,
Japanese aid, Nagasu noted, is aimed at promoting exports, expanding
overseas markets, increasing overseas private direct investments, and
securing raw materials. Fourth, he maintained, the aid has increasingly been used for the establishment of a monopolistic Japanese
capitalist system and for the pursuit of a collective imperial security
system in Asia centering around an alliance between the United States
and Japan. Fifth, he noted, Japanese aid has been given to one camp
of divided nations, consisting of South Korea, Taiwan, and South
Vietnam, and to such countries as Thailand, Indonesia, and the Philippines. These countries form part of the group supported by the United
States in the postwar era of East-West confrontation. Sixth, according
to Nagasu, the transformation of Japanese aid motives has taken place
in recent years; the primary motive continues to be expansion of exports, but it is increasingly aimed at directing exports to third countries. The encouragement of overseas direct private investment
Nagasu noted, is tied to a "labor motive" as a result of an increasing
shortage of labor in Japan. In addition to these reasons, Nagasu
noted, the Japanese government and business leaders are concerned
with securing mineral and energy resources from abroad, for which
an enormous amount of Japanese capital will be distributed in the
form of foreign aid. Furthermore, he pointed out, the establishment of
factories outside Japan is expected to take place, with environmental
considerations restricting further unlimited heavy industrialization
of the Japanese homeland. Nagasu also contended that Japanese aid
merely allows for the flow of capital out of Japan. Finally, based on
this understanding of Japanese aid, Nagasu hinted that there is a
possibility of Japan making a new attempt to bring about a military
solution, similar to the prewar Japanese scheme, in order to secure
adequate supplies of natural resources. [12]

Halliday and McCormack were more blunt than Nagasu: they
equated the efforts of the postwar Japanese leaders directly with those
of the prewar Japanese capitalist and militarist leaders who had tried,
but failed, to create by the use of force a "Greater East Asia Co-
prosperity Sphere." The postwar Japanese capitalists, according to
Halliday and McCormack, have changed their tactics, but not their
strategy, for Asian domination—aid is used merely as a tool to realize
such domination. Viewed in this context, aid loans, credits, and
investments are seen as measures to facilitate increased Japanese
take-over of the factors of production available in neighboring countries. [13]

Kawata, on the other hand, observed that the process of katagawari (mentioned above) has been taking place since the United States began reducing her involvement in Asia. The Vietnam War weakened the economic position of the United States, Kawata noted, while it enabled Japan to expand her exports and overseas investments in Asian countries, resulting in increased Japanese presence and influence in the area. There remains, according to Kawata, the danger of a revival of Japanese militarism for the sake of protecting Japanese economic interests that have been built up in Asia.[14]

Advocates of the self-preservationist view of foreign aid have also recognized the prominence of economic motives in Japanese aid. They admit that the Japanese government has been actively concerned with protecting the immediate economic interests of the country; they insist, however, that this has been done out of necessity. They believe the primary objective of Japanese aid, like the objectives of Japan's other national policies, is to ensure the survival or self-preservation of Japan. For this reason, they note aid is provided not only to sell Japanese products abroad but to secure raw materials, mineral products, and energy resources that Japan lacks decisively. Kazuo Nishi, for example, noted how baisho (reparations) payments, export credits, and development loans had first been designed to help in the reconstruction and growth of the Japanese economy, but that the Japanese government then shifted its aid policy to secure ample supplies of raw materials and natural resources.[15]

The self-preservationist view has been advanced by Saburo Okita in terms of Japan's dependency on natural resources as being a decisive element in the formation of Japanese foreign policy. Noting that Japan cannot attain self-sufficiency in energy without drastically reducing its level of economic activity and standard of living, Okita suggested that Japan take such steps as diversifying its resources supply, cooperating with resource exporting countries, modifying its industrial structure, encouraging a saving of resources among its populace, and reducing its rate of economic growth. As Japan remains happo-yabure, or defenseless on all sides because of her complete dependence on imports of raw materials, energy, and foodstuffs, Okita considered it unrealistic in Japan to dream of attempting self-sufficiency. Instead he suggested the aforementioned measures, as well as increased economic cooperation with other nations.[16]

The doctrine of world communalism in foreign aid has not yet become an influential one among aid policy makers in Japan. Since being initially advocated by the Pearson Commission in 1969, however, it has become a popular theme discussed widely among Japanese academic circles. Advocates of this theme have called for a redirection of Japanese aid toward reducing the gap between rich and poor countries. Their concept resembles that of Myrdal; the objective of foreign aid is seen as one of reducing poverty and improving the welfare of people in poor countries in a similar manner to what has been attempted domestically in Japan. The improvement of living conditions in less-developed countries is therefore regarded as a task for all of the countries of the world including Japan. [17]

Such an interpretation of the role of foreign aid has been forcefully presented by Akira Onishi, who viewed development assistance within the framework of chikyuka, or globalization. In Onishi's view the world once consisted of nation-states that competed to assert their own nationalism; it was at that time advantageous to follow the overall policy of developing one's own country and strengthening her military forces. For example in the 1950s and 1960s, Onishi noted, foreign aid programs were used for the attainment of political objectives and the protection of economic interests. But, he pointed out, the world is now passing from the era of nationalism and conflict among nation-states into a new era emphasizing a world community based on a commonly shared sense of the interdependence of its member nations. In this light Onishi suggested that Japanese aid policy be aimed at the creation of a harmonious and efficient international society and a global welfare state based on a clear understanding that the earth is one, and that development assistance be considered a "necessary social responsibility cost in the era of globalization. "[18]

While the five contemporary views of aid outlined above highlight certain characteristic aspects of Japanese aid, they remain individually partial, and thus fall short of explaining comprehensively the objectives and nature of Japanese aid. To understand these fully, then, there is a need to adopt some of the points made by each contemporary view and integrate them into a single comprehensive view. Such a view is presented below; it is labeled a historical national evolutionalist view.

HISTORICAL NATIONAL EVOLUTIONALIST VIEW

The historical national evolutionalist view, presented for the first time in this study, maintains that Japanese aid is provided to help attain Japan's evolving national goals, ultimately directed to achieving Japan's societal welfare and her international ascendancy. According to this view, Japanese aid is seen as an instrument of Japan's national policy to serve the kokueki, or national interest, of "secularized postwar Japan."

Kokueki and "secularized postwar Japan" are two concepts which allow for fuller comprehension of the uniqueness or peculiarity of Japanese aid in its totality. The concept of kokueki, in particular, helps define Japan's objectives in relation to its national goals, and the concept of "secularized postwar Japan" helps distinguish Japan's postwar national goals and policies from those of prewar Japan. The objectives and nature of Japanese foreign aid can then be seen in its historical perspective as an instrument of Japan's evolving national policy.

Since 1868, when Japan entered her modern era following the Meiji restoration, she has held essentially three national goals: national security, modernization and development, and the attainment of a high status among leading world powers. In her efforts to fulfill these goals Japan has had to fight against a lack of adequate domestic land and natural resources preventing her from sustaining economic activities and environmental conditions at levels desired by the Japanese. Meanwhile, the nature of these national goals, and the means used to attain them, have changed, particularly before and after World War II. The goals were transformed from those of politico-military imperialism in the prewar era to those of economic nationalism in the postwar era.

While Western powers were colonizing most of Asia, and threatening Japan, in the nineteenth century, the Japanese had put as their primary goal the independence and security of their homeland. But after the Meiji government had consolidated its forces and expelled the foreign powers, it embarked upon the task of modernizing and developing Japan. Modernization at that time meant primarily the centralization of political power, and economic development was characterized by industrialization. The modernization plan was aimed at fukoku kyohei, or the enrichment of Japan and the strengthening of her forces for two ultimate goals: to secure Japan's place among the leading world powers, or rekkyo koku, and to establish her own empire.

During the postwar era (from the end of World War II in 1945 to the return of Okinawa to Japan and to the visit by former President Nixon to China in 1972) the Japanese looked upon the world's leading nations, or sensin koku, in terms of high gross national product and high per capita income. Relying exclusively on the United States for her security from external threats, the Japanese in the postwar era concentrated their efforts on economic development and growth; this meant raising both their gross national product and per capita income. Thus while economic development was directed for the purpose of fukoku kyohei in the prewar era, the economic objective became an end in itself in the postwar period. Japan's primary national goal had therefore shifted from imperial domination (in the prewar era) to domestic prosperity (in the postwar era), and from politico-military imperialism to economic nationalism.

This study will not give a detailed discussion of Japanese ways of thinking. [19] Instead it will highlight, below, certain conceptual differences in the prewar and postwar Japanese views of social nexus and in the national goals of Japan, in order to clearly indicate the direction in which Japan's national policy has been placed, and to analyze Japan's aid program as an instrument of her national policy designed to attain her basic goals. For these purposes four related components of Japanese thought will be examined: kokutai, kokueki,

daitowa kyoeiken, and sekai kyodotai, and in particular, the conceptual differences of daitowa kyoeiken and sekai kyodotai will be distin-
guished.

The concept of kokutai embodied the essence of Japanese social
nexus. The term that was used most frequently in the prewar era may
be translated as national essence or national policy. It had three
meanings: first, that Japan is a unique nation-state ruled by its
sovereign, the emperor; second, that the whole of Japan was regarded
as a big family consisting of members devoted to their collective
welfare; and third, that the Japanese nation consisted of social components that were inherently unequal, but were placed in certain
"proper" positions to undertake tasks necessary for the well-being
of the Japanese society. [20] The government made every effort to
indoctrinate the people with the idea of kokutai, thus almost compelling the people to believe in the uniqueness and righteousness of
Japan and to work for the country by devoting their lives to it. As a
result of the implementation of the kokutai idea with the adoption of
advanced technology brought in from abroad, Japan became a modern
centralized and industrialized state, but at the same time dependent
on supplies of raw materials and mineral resources from abroad. As
Kazushi Ohkawa and Henry Rosovsky noted, the Japanese economy
contained, in the middle of the 1880s, a growing modern sector
consisting of cotton textile and other light manufacturing industries
based upon imported raw materials and machinery; but by the beginning
of the twentieth century the economy had greatly expanded its scale,
requiring both increased imports of raw materials and increased exports
of its products to foreign markets. [21]

The successful creation of a modern Japanese state convinced
Japanese leaders of the prewar era of the need to spread the domain
of Japanese policy over the rest of Asia. This belief, and the desire
to control overseas markets and sources of raw materials and natural
resources, resulted in the development of the plan for daitowa kyoeiken,
or the "Greater East Asia Co-prosperity Sphere. " This was not just
a simple plan for the liberation of Asia from Western colonialism,
nor was it a mere proposal to create what is presently known as a
common market. According to the plan, Asia was to become a state
ruled by the Japanese emperor with divine power. The daitowa kyoeiken
plan, however, received neither sympathy nor understanding from the
indigenous populations that would have been placed in their "proper"
positions had they been included in the Japanese empire.

The defeat of Japan in World War II, brought the disappearance
of the most significant component of kokutai—the existence of a
unique Japanese state governed by a divine emperor. The kokutai
concept was then replaced by the doctrine of kokueki, which may be
translated as the interest of the country or national interest. In
essence kokueki represented the national interest of the secularized
kokutai, thereby still holding two other components of the Japanese

society. The protection of kokueki meant continuous efforts made by
the Japanese to attain their national goals under changing domestic
and foreign conditions.

The basic national goals of secularized postwar Japan were,
again, essentially the same as those of prewar Japan: security,
development, and ascendancy. They were different only in the order
of their priorities and in the extent of efforts made by the Japanese
for their attainment. In the postwar era, as before, Japan gave primary
importance to her security from external threats, but actually took
little action in this direction, for three reasons. First, the Japanese,
since their defeat in World War II, have held a generally strong antipathy toward any action smacking of militarism. They have followed a
policy of upholding Article 9 of the new Japanese Constitution, which
prohibits not only the use of force as a means of settling international
disputes but even the creation and maintenance of armed forces.
Article 9, which may sound a bit utopian, declares:

> Aspiring sincerely to an international peace based on justice
> and order, the Japanese people forever renounce war as a
> sovereign right of the nation and the threat or use of force as
> means of settling international disputes.
> In order to accomplish the aim of the preceding paragraph,
> land, sea and air forces, as well as other war potential, will
> never be maintained. The right of belligerency of the state
> will not be recognized. [22]

The government of Japan has indeed built up Japanese military
forces in the name of the inherent right of self-defense. But it has
continued to encounter a great deal of difficulty in increasing the
strength of these "self-defense" forces, finding widespread public
antipathy and opposition not only from opposing political parties but
from the majority of the Japanese people as well.

The second reason that Japan has taken little action to further
its national security is that the countries of Asia, remembering their
past experiences under Japanese military rule, fear any revival
of Japanese militarism, and have not particularly sought military
assistance from Japan. Neither did they strongly urge the participation of Japan in such regional security arrangements as the Southeast
Asia Treaty Organization (SEATO). For her part Japan refrained from
intervening in disputes between neighboring countries, lest she
would be accused of fomenting a modern sanitized version of the
prewar "Greater East Asia Co-prosperity Sphere."

Third, as noted above, Japan has relied exclusively on the United
States for her defense against external threats. In fact Japan has
excluded any other possible means to safeguard her security. Her
total dependence on the United States in this respect is further
epitomized by the San Francisco peace treaty that Japan signed in

1951 at the direction of the United States, and by the mutual security treaties which Japan concluded with the United States in 1951 and 1960, and which were extended indefinitely in 1970.

With this dependence on the United States, Japan, as mentioned above, could turn her efforts in the direction of domestic prosperity, international recognition, and a higher place among the world's communities. That she put economic development and growth at the forefront of these goals was noted by Okita:

> After the serious disillusionment about the policy of milita-
> ristic expansion and the misery and devastation people
> experienced due to the bankruptcy of this policy, the Japa-
> nese people in general have tended to assume an "economy
> first" attitude. The energy of the people, dissipated in mili-
> tary actions in the past, is now concentrated upon economic
> rehabilitation and development. Business is now attracting
> the best brain among young people and the ability and energy
> of scientists and engineers is now fully applied to the produc-
> tion and improvement of civilian commodities. [23]

Thus the Japanese single-mindedly devoted their energy to the economic growth and development of their country. Once the rehabilitation of the Japanese economy had been accomplished, within several years after the end of World War II, it grew at the average rate of 10 percent a year to become the third largest economy in the world by the beginning of the 1970s.

With the return of sovereignty to Japan, Japanese foreign aid was launched in the early 1950s. The aid program set up by the Japanese was tailored to attain five objectives that are ultimately related to Japan's basic national goals: (1) to spur the process of Japanese reconstruction and economic growth; (2) to establish diplomatic rela-tions between Japan and neighboring countries; (3) to maintain a political, economic, and social system, and to stabilize policies of aid-receiving countries that are beneficial to Japan; (4) to raise per capita income in Japan; and (5) to assert Japan's influence and leader-ship in both regional and global communities.

The relative importance and priorities given to the five objectives have changed over the two decades since the initiation of the aid program. During the program's 10 years Japan sought to provide aid resources to achieve a reentry into the international community con-sisting of countries maintaining political and economic systems similar to that of Japan. Her aid program, consisting mainly of reparations payments, was also used to help certain industries complete their recovery from devastation by the war. During the program's second 10 years, economic motives and objectives became the main factors shaping Japanese aid policies. As Japan benefited from the existing international system, she worked to strengthen her ties with friendly governments and to stabilize their policies that were favorable to Japanese economic expansion. By the middle of the 1960s Japan had established her position as an important member of the non-Communist world. Then in an effort to gain recognition as a leader in the international community, she began expanding the geographic and sectoral coverage of her aid program.

Meanwhile Japan's successful heavy industrialization and overseas economic expansion brought three far-reaching consequences ultimately necessitating fundamental changes in the nature of Japan's basic national goals and corresponding modifications in the objectives of the Japanese foreign aid program in the late 1960s and early 1970s. First, there developed a growing share of Japanese business throughout the world, causing envy and fear among other countries. Second, there was, as noted previously, an ever-increasing Japanese need for imports of raw materials and energy resources from abroad, making Japan almost entirely dependent on resource-rich countries. Third, there was the aforementioned deterioration of environmental conditions in Japan, requiring not only a slowdown in further heavy industrial activity but a basic change in Japan's industrial structure.

As Japan's share of imports and exports increased in almost every other country, Japanese economic power became increasingly envied and feared. As Karel Holbik noted: "In the eyes of the Asian LDC's [less-developed countries], Japan has grown to be 'Colossus of the North' in the Asian context. To the United States, Japan became a dollar-hoarding creditor."[24] Both less-developed and developed countries in fact began to demand that Japan implement measures to minimize any adverse impact, and maximize any favorable outcome, of Japanese economic expansion abroad. Japan's response to these international demands and her approach to reorienting her national goals were symptomatic of the Japanese society. As a nation in the international community Japan acted as the Japanese would have acted in their own country. Japan was now seen as a member of wider entities called respectively chiiki kyodotai (a regional community) or sekai kyodotai (a world community). Japan's conduct in these communities was governed by two elements of Japanese thought: her desire to get along with other nations for the sake of preserving the collective interest of these communities, and her understanding of the communities as consisting of essentially unequal members effectively working together in their various stations according to their ability to contribute to the community.

The desire to get along with other nations constituted an effective force to compel Japan to accept many of the recommendations on aid policies made by such international bodies as the United Nations Conference on Trade and Development (UNCTAD), OECD, and the Pearson Commission. Given the Japanese way of thinking, emphasizing social cooperation as a basic structure, it was considered within Japan's kokueki to take into account what other nations may have thought and said of Japan. Japan became particularly receptive to criticism by other advanced countries as she sought to be regarded as one of these countries. As will be described in Chapter 2, this Japanese thinking led to the adoption of a policy which may informally be called otsukiai, meaning that Japan would do what others expected of her in the conduct of her international relations, including the extension of aid to less-developed countries.

In line with their understanding of communities consisting of unequal members, the Japanese tended to regard the advancement of less-developed countries as a secondary objective of Japan's foreign aid. In the Japanese view a nation can improve its own living conditions only through self-reliance and self-help. [25] Therefore, while Japanese foreign aid was treated conceptually as a means of assisting its recipient nations in their self-reliance efforts, in reality the aid program was used mostly to realize Japan's potential for her own development and attainment of a proper place in regional and world communities. This primary concern with Japan's own kokueki along with her marginal interest in the welfare of aid-receiving countries, caused a growing discrepancy between what Japan claimed to be doing with her foreign aid and what she actually did with it. Her "Japan's interest first" approach in fact was seen to stir bitter resentment among some of the countries receiving Japanese aid; these countries had strong desires of their own to establish national economic integration and economic independence, and they began demanding that their interest be placed first in the formulation and implementation of the Japanese aid program.

The second cause for a change in the nature of Japan's national goals and in the objectives of her foreign aid emerged gradually as a result of her continuing efforts in heavy industrialization. As the gross national product of Japan grew to a magnitude comparable to that of European nations by the mid-1960s, Japan's national goal began to be directed to the attainment of a level of per capita income equal to that of European nations and, eventually, to that of the United States. She attempted to reach this goal through continued economic growth centering around further heavy industrialization. Such efforts required ever-increasing supplies of raw materials and mineral and energy resources not only from neighboring Asian countries but from all over the world. Thus Japan used her foreign aid program more to expand her contacts with resource-rich countries than to help resource-poor less developed countries which needed assistance most.

NOTES

1. The importance scholars attach to ascertaining aid objectives and motives is seen in the fact that these studies commonly start

13

with an identification of the objectives and motives regardless of
their fields of discipline. John D. Montgomery, The Politics of
Foreign Aid (New York: Praeger, 1962), pp. 11-60; Goran Ohlin,
Foreign Aid Policies Reconsidered (Paris: OECD Development Center,
1966), pp. 13-54; and Raymond F. Mikesell, The Economics of Foreign
Aid (Chicago: Aldine, 1968), pp. 1-26.

2. Robert S. Walters, American and Soviet Aid (Pittsburgh:
University of Pittsburgh Press, 1970), pp. 8-48.

3. Lester Pearson et al., Partners in Development (New York:
Praeger, 1969), p. 8.

4. Ohlin, op. cit., pp. 44-48.

5. Gunnar Myrdal, Challenge of World Poverty (New York: Vintage
Books, 1969), p. 365.

6. Yoichi Itagaki, "Namboku Mondai to Ekonomikku Nashonarism,"
Namboku Mondai, ed. Yoichi Itagaki (Tokyo: Toyo Keizai Shimpo Sha,
1971), pp. 1-34.

7. John White, Japanese Aid (London: Overseas Development
Institute, 1964).

8. Ohlin, op. cit., p. 30.

9. Leon Hollerman, Japan's Dependence on the World Economy
(Princeton, N. J.: Princeton University Press, 1967), p. 199.

10. Samuel P. Huntington, "Foreign Aid: For What and for
Whom?," Development Today, ed. Robert E. Hunter and John E.
Rielly, (New York: Praeger, 1972), p. 28.

11. United States Department of Agriculture, Japanese Overseas
Aid and Investments: Their Potential Effects on World and U. S. Farm
Exports (Washington: Government Printing Office, 1972), p. 20.

12. Kazuji Nagasu, Nanshin suru Nippon Shihon Shugi (Tokyo:
Mainichi Shimbun Sha, 1971), pp. 348-61.

13. John Halliday and Gavan McCormack, Japanese Imperialism
Today—Co-Prosperity in Greater East Asia (London: Penguin Books,
1973).

14. Tadashi Kawata, Sho Nippon Shugi no Susume (Tokyo:
Daiyamondo Sha, 1972).

15. Kazuo Nishi, Keizai Kyoryoku (Tokyo: Chuo Koran Sha,
1970).

16. Saburo Okita, "Natural Resource Dependency and Japanese
Foreign Policy," Foreign Affairs, vol. 52, no. 4 (July 1974), pp. 714-
24.

17. Saburo Okita, Ekonomisto no Yakuwari (Tokyo: Nippon
Keizai Shimbun Sha, 1973), pp. 109-44.

18. Akira Onishi, Kaihatsu Enjo (Tokyo: Nippon Keizai Shimbun
Sha, 1973), pp. 9-17.

19. Hajime Nakamura, Ways of Thinking of Eastern Peoples:
India, China, Tibet, Japan (Honolulu: East-West Center Press, 1964),
pp. 343-587 and Chie Nakane, Japanese Society (Berkeley: University
of California Press, 1970).

20. See Nobutaka Iko, Japanese Politics (New York: Alfred Knopf, 1957), pp. 38-49. The interpretation of the term is that of the author.

21. Kazushi Ohkawa and Henry Rosovsky, "A Century of Japanese Economic Growth, " The State and Economic Enterprise in Japan, ed. William Lockwood (Princeton University Press, 1965), p. 59.

22. Edwin O. Reischbauer, The United States and Japan (New York: Viking Press, 1965), p. 351.

23. Saburo Okita, Causes and Problems of Rapid Growth in Post-war Japan and Their Implications for Newly Developing Countries (Tokyo: Japan Economic Research Center, 1967), pp. 20-21.

24. Karel Holbik, "Japan: Economic Growth and Foreign Aid, " Intereconomics no. 10, 1973, p. 308. (Hamburg: Verlag Waltarchiv GMBH, 1973).

25. Speech delivered by Kiichi Aichi, Japan's chief delegate to the Santiago session of UNCTAD on April 14, 1972; Japan, Ministry of Foreign Affairs, Japan and Asian Development (Tokyo: 1972), p. 8.

2

The Japanese government has claimed that Japan has been extending aid to less-developed countries, for their socio-economic development, in spite of Japan's own limited resources and domestic requirements.[1] It has at the same time conceded that Japan extended aid for a number of other reasons aimed ultimately at the attainment of Japan's own changing national goals. For example in the beginning of the 1960s the Japanese government asserted that Japanese aid was extended to enable the recipient countries to buy more Japanese goods and to promote Japan's own "political security."[2] Several years later, in 1967, Japan declared that the objective of its aid program was the advancement of less-developed countries, because such advancement was essential for the maintenance of both international peace and a viable world economy. According to the Japanese government, international peace and a viable world economy constituted a necessary condition for the continued economic prosperity of Japan.[3] By 1973 Japan was said to have become convinced of the need to expand her aid because it was her responsibility to do so as an advanced member of the international community.[4]

This chapter will describe how the official Japanese aid policies have evolved over a period of a little more than twenty years, and will identify the various aid measures that the Japanese government has claimed to have taken during this period. The evolution of Japanese foreign aid is divided into five major phases according to the transformation that has taken place in the objectives and role of Japanese aid as a result of changes in the nature and priority of Japan's national goals.

The first phase runs from 1952, when Japan regained her sovereignty, to 1956, when the Hatoyama government was dissolved and Japan was admitted to the United Nations. This period includes the Yoshida, Hatoyama, and Ishibashi administrations, during which the Japanese government claimed that Japan extended economic and tech-

nical assistance in spite of her own domestic requirements for both
capital and technology. The government stressed the fact that Japanese
private investments in less-developed countries had increased from
$2.9 million in 1951 to $18 million in 1956. It also mentioned, as
further proof of Japan's intention to undertake global economic cooperation, the establishment in 1950 of the Export Bank of Japan, which
was followed by the bank's reorganization as the Export-Import Bank
of Japan two years later. The baisho (reparations) payments were cited
by the government as contributing significantly to the economic development of the recipient countries. Moreover the Japanese pointed
proudly to a host of international agencies and programs in which
Japan was participating in the 1950s—the United Nations Expanded
Program of Technical Assistance (EPTA), the International Bank for
Reconstruction and Development (the World Bank), the International
Monetary Fund (IMF), the United Nations Economic Commission for
Asia and the Far East (ECAFE), and the Colombo Plan. [5]

The second phase of Japanese foreign aid runs from 1957, when
Kishi became prime minister, until the end of the Ikeda administration
in 1964. Both Kishi and Ikeda looked upon Asia as a potential contributor to Japan's economic growth and expansion. They saw Asia as
an area in which Japan could take strong economic leadership. For
Kishi and Ikeda, attempts to conclude separate peace treaties with
certain countries of Asia became just one of several activities related
to what the Japanese began to call keizai kyoyoku mondai, or economic
cooperation matters. During this second phase the objectives of Japanese aid were designated as the expansion of Japanese export markets
and the stabilization of the socio-economic and political systems of
recipient countries, which ultimately would contribute to Japan's own
political security.

The fact that the promotion of exports of Japanese products was
the main concern of the Japanese government during the second phase
of the aid program is clearly seen in an aid policy statement issued
by Japan's Ministry of Foreign Affairs (Gaimusho) in 1961. Noting
that Japan depended largely on exports for her existence, Gaimusho
publicly admitted Japan's desire to increase the capacity of less-
developed countries to import various goods, thereby expanding
Japanese exports and helping Japan attain one of her key national
goals, a doubling of Japanese national income within ten years;
Japanese foreign aid was thus directly linked to a national policy
objective. The Gaimusho statement noted:

> Japan depends on the markets of less-developed countries
> for close to 45 percent of her exports and imports. Her trade
> with Southeast Asia and other newly developing areas amounts
> to approximately 10 percent of her gross national product. It
> is natural, therefore, that Japan, which must trade to live,
> has a vital interest in the steady economic development of

Southeast Asia and other less-developed regions and the expansion thereby of their external purchasing powers. For example, Japan's new ten-year plan to double the country's national income by the end of the plan period (1961-1970) envisages a 10 percent annual increase over the base year in the total volume of her exports with an average of 13 percent annual increase in the exports of heavy industrial products. Such rates of increase of her exports can hardly be achieved without a steady rise in the capacity of less-developed countries to import. [6]

As noted above the second objective of Japanese aid during this phase of the program was the protection of Japan's own political security. As the gap between rich and poor became increasingly wider in newly independent nations, the Japanese government regarded this as a potential threat to Japan's prosperity and security. Both Kishi and Ikeda agreed on the desirability of strengthening Japan's relations with those countries that maintained a political and socio-economic system similar to that of Japan. A further statement issued by Gaimusho reveals the Japanese policy makers' perception of the imminent danger to Japan's security:

Moreover, the existing gap in newly developing countries between the peoples' pressing desire for higher standards of living and their abysmal misery in daily life, if left to widen further, will eventually breed among them resentment and disillusionment (of the present system), leading to political and social instability. Should this happen in Asia, it can be harmful to Japan's own political security which largely depends on the stability of her Asian neighbors. [7]

To help less-developed countries resolve their socio-economic problems, Japan was said to be taking a number of specific aid measures. The measures mentioned were government loans and credits, grants such as the baisho payments, technical assistance, investments, and contributions to various multilateral aid programs. As specific examples of Japanese aid Gaimusho cited credits to India and Pakistan, loans to Indonesia and the Philippines, increased private overseas investments, technical training programs developed in cooperation with the Colombo Plan, and contributions to such multilateral organizations and programs as EPTA, U.N. Special Fund, the Asian Productivity Organization, (APO), and the World Bank. Gaimusho at the same time noted that Japan had become a member of the Development Assistance Group (DAG) of the Organization for European Economic Cooperation and Development (OECD) in 1964. Gaimusho also emphasized that Japan had strengthened her administrative mechanism by establishing the Overseas Economic Cooperation Fund (OECF) in 1961 and the Overseas Technical Cooperation Agency (OTCA) in 1962.

By the middle of the 1960s, when the third phase of Japanese aid was launched, Japan was said to have become concerned with possible adverse effects of the miserable state of socio-economic conditions in less-developed countries on the developed countries as a whole, including Japan. Rapid population increases and shortages of capital and industrial know-how were seen as the main causes of the relatively slow development of less-developed countries. The Japanese government during this period declared that Japan was providing aid because "without political stability and economic growth in these areas of the world, neither the prosperity of the developed countries nor the welfare of the people of the world, as a whole, can be achieved with satisfaction."[8]

As token proof of Japanese concern, Japan accepted the recommendations made by the United Nations Conference on Trade and Development (UNCTAD) in 1964, and by the Development Assistance Committee (DAC) of OECD in 1965, that 1 percent of national income of the developed countries be set aside for assistance to less-developed countries. Japan did not set any target date for reaching the recommended level. However, the government said efforts would be made by the Japanese to reach the target in spite of the low per capita income in Japan and the existence of numerous other domestic problems that needed urgent attention by the government. In addition the government asserted it was taking steps to ease the terms of Japanese aid loans to relieve the recipients of their high debt servicing; to emphasize aid to such neighboring countries as Korea and Taiwan, and on Southeast Asian countries; to foster agricultural development in the recipient countries; to implement preferential treatment for the import of raw materials and goods produced in less-developed countries; and to promote regional and multilateral cooperative activities.[9]

Japanese aid was also reportedly directed to raising agricultural productivity, because the Japanese government believed increased output would help less-developed countries deal more effectively with the problem of feeding their own rapidly expanding population. Japan was said to be in the best position to extend technical assistance on rice cultivation, as a result of her accumulation of experience and technical skill and know-how. Lack of technical infrastructure was said to constitute as great a limiting factor for the development of less-developed countries as their lack of capital. Confident of Japan's industrial techniques, which had made possible rapid reconstruction of the Japanese economy after World War II, the government claimed that it intended to expand technical assistance in future years.[10]

In citing Japan's role in multilateral assistance programs, Gaimusho made repeated reference to Japan's participation in the consortia set up in the late 1950s for India and Pakistan. It also

19

noted the active role played by Japan in the Mekong Committee, the Asian Development Bank, the Foreign Exchange Operations Fund for Laos, and the Inter-Governmental Group for Indonesia. Moreover, to promote regional cooperation, the Japanese government claimed, Japan had formed the Ministerial Conference for the Economic Development of Southeast Asia in 1966. The conference was claimed to have offered a forum for discussions between the developing and developed countries of Asia. [11]

In the early 1970s, when the fourth stage of Japanese aid was begun, Japan reportedly became convinced of the need to further expand global economic cooperation because, Japan said, both her security and domestic prosperity depended on international peace and prosperity in general. In an address to the Diet in January 1972, Prime Minister Sato declared that he intended to actively strengthen Japan's foreign aid to help solve namboku mondai, or "north-south problems," described as one of the major challenges facing the world. [12] Kiichi Aichi, Japan's chief delegate to the 1972 UNCTAD talks in Santiago, reiterated Japan's aid policy:

Peace in the world and prosperity in the developing areas of the world are indispensable to the peace and prosperity of my country. Fully conscious of such realities and dedicated to peace, my country is firmly determined to intensify its contributions to international cooperation for development. [13]

As specific policy measures to expand international cooperation, Aichi said, Japan would (1) ensure an overall flow of financial resources to developing nations equal to one percent of her gross national product) by 1975; (2) increase the volume of her official development assistance to 0.7 percent of her gross national product; (3) improve the terms of her official development assistance to meet the target set by DAC in 1969 (see Chapter 3); (4) expand grants, technical assistance, and contributions to international organizations; (5) make efforts to expand the untying of bilateral government aid loans and, as well, examine the possibility of implementing a complete untying of loans on a unilateral basis before an international agreement is reached on a general untying; (6) promote private investments to contribute to the industrial growth of the developing countries; and (7) give particular attention to the least developed among the developing countries within the framework of the United Nations Development Programme (UNDP), either by earmarking certain funds for them or establishing a special fund. [14]

Japanese government leaders at the same time began to mention "Japan's responsibility" as an advanced member of sekai kyodotai, (the world community). In his administrative speech in January 1973, Prime Minister Tanaka became the first Japanese leader to reveal the pride held by many of his countrymen in Japan's attainment of an influential position in the international community as a result of her expanded efforts over the quarter of a century since the end of World War II. Tanaka said that it was both a global request and Japan's responsibility toward the international community to provide assistance by making available to developing nations Japan's economic and technical resources, thereby promoting in these nations self-help and self-reliance (ejiritsu jijo) efforts as well as social stability. Tanaka's foreign minister, Masayoshi Ohira, similarly advocated the expansion of Japanese assistance to developing countries as one of the main priority areas of Japanese foreign policy and as a means to help developing countries help themselves. [15]

NOTES

1. See Gaimusho, (Ministry of Foreign Affairs) Waga Gaiko no kinkyo and Tsusansho, (Ministry of International Trade and Industry) Keizai kyoryoku no Genjo to Mondait-ten, published annually, for official explanation and assessment of Japanese aid policies.

2. Japan, Ministry of Foreign Affairs, Some Features of Japan's Development Assistance (Tokyo: 1961), p. 1.

3. Japan, Ministry of Foreign Affairs, Japan's Foreign Aid (Tokyo: 1967).

4. Administrative speech delivered by Prime Minister Tanaka in January 1973; see Gaimusho, Waga Gaiko no kinkyo: Showa 48-nen Do (Tokyo: 1973), pp. 432-41.

5. Kajima Heiwa Kenkyujo, ed., Nippon no Keizai Kyoryoku (Tokyo: Kajima Heiwa Kenkyujo Shuppan Kai, 1973), pp. 39-41.

6. Japan, Ministry of Foreign Affairs, Some Features of Japan's Development Assistance op. cit., p. 1.

7. Ibid.

8. Japan, Ministry of Foreign Affairs, Japan's Foreign Aid, op. cit., p. 1.

9. Ibid., pp. 2-6.

10. Japan, Ministry of Foreign Affairs, Japan's Foreign Aid op. cit., pp. 7-8.

11. Ibid., pp. 8-11.

12. Gaimusho, Waga Gaiko no Kinkyo: Showa 47 nen ban (Tokyo: 1972), p. 417.

13. Japan, Ministry of Foreign Affairs, Japan and Asian Development (Tokyo: 1972), p. 8.

14. Ibid., pp. 7-15.

15. Gaimusho, Waga Gaiko no Kinkyo: Showa 48-nen Do (Tokyo: 1973), pp. 432-33.

3

COMPOSITION
AND MAGNITUDE OF
JAPANESE AID RESOURCES

As noted in Chapter 2, the Japanese government officially pledged that Japan would provide, for the purpose of development assistance, 1 percent of her gross national product (GNP) by 1975. In practice the overall flow of financial resources from Japan to less-developed countries and to multilateral organizations, as measured by the Development Assistance Group (DAG), increased steadily after 1955, and surpassed the target level in 1973. This steady growth in the overall Japanese aid flow took place mainly on the strength of a rapid increase in the flow of private resources through export and import credits and through private direct and portfolio investments. This chapter will examine, first, the composition and magnitude of Japanese aid resources and, second, the extent of genuineness of Japanese aid, that is, the levels and percentages of resources that can reasonably be considered as genuine aid.

COMPOSITION

Japanese foreign aid consists of activities that Japan carries out to induce the transfer of both physical resources and technical know-how from Japan to recipient countries through bilateral and multilateral channels, for the purpose of bringing about what Japan considers a desirable continuation or, or a change in, certain policies of the recipient countries for the ultimate fulfillment of Japan's kokueki (national interest) and the attainment of her national goals. This definition of Japanese aid should be clarified according to the terminology and concepts it employs, namely, (1) Japan as a donor, (2) "physical resources" and "technical know-how," (3) "recipient countries," (4) the notion of "sacrifice," (5) the manner in which aid resources are channeled, and (6) the (already stated) objective of Japanese aid.

The term "Japan as a donor" of aid encompasses both Japanese government agencies and private entities. The government agencies and private entities, notably business establishments, carry out close consultations in formulating Japan's aid policy. With few exceptions, Japanese aid plans and intentions that are publicly revealed by government officials represent the outcome of consensus-building deliberations carried out by representatives of dominant political, bureaucratic, business, and academic groups. In the implementation of her aid policy Japan as a donor also relies not only on her public institutions and agencies for capital and technical assistance activities, but on private businesses for the providing of credits and investments. [1]

Official aid resources include all funds made available to recipient countries either directly or indirectly by Japanese government agencies; official aid resources also include funds extended by Japanese government agencies to private institutions and to international aid agencies. The baisho that Japan paid to several Southeast Asian countries following the end of World War II are also treated as part of Japanese aid; there are three reasons for this. First, the San Francisco peace treaty of 1951 allowed Japan to negotiate with each claimant country on the magnitude and content of the baisho payments. Japan was not required by the treaty to pay any fixed amount of predetermined goods or services. Second, as Robert S. Ozaki noted, the effect of reparations payments on recipient countries turned out to be essentially the same as that of aid flows. [2] Third, the baisho constituted a burden to the Japanese economy that, as will be discussed in Chapter 4, was the largest grant component of Japanese aid in its early stages. Moreover the baisho has been included as part of development assistance by the Development Assistance Committee (DAC) of the Organization for Economic Cooperation and Development (OECD) in its assessment of the aid policies of its members.

The terms "physical resources" and "technical know-how" are used to refer to actual goods and services delivered to the recipient countries. These include the services of technical assistance experts and commodities such as consumer goods. [3]

The term "recipient countries" is used to cite countries that have received as aid from Japan physical resources and/or technical assistance. The People's Republic of China, for example, is excluded from the list of recipients of Japanese aid, although she has received export credit and loans from Japan at concessional terms. [4] This exclusion is due to the fact that China has declared herself a less-developed country and a member of the Third World, but not part of the group of countries receiving aid or assistance. China in fact did not receive substantial assistance from other countries for at least ten years after the withdrawal of Soviet aid in the late 1950s. Nor has China accepted any assistance from multilateral U.N. aid agencies, including the World Bank. The flow of resources between

Japan and China is considered as involving two countries with equal status. The Republic of China (Taiwan), on the other hand, is included in this study as one of the recipients of Japanese aid, although her per capita income has risen steadily and has certainly become higher than that of Mainland China. There are two main reasons for the inclusion of Taiwan in the list of aid recipients: Taiwan has received development assistance loans and credits from Japan, and multilateral agencies have extended funds to Taiwan on concessional terms.

The notion of "sacrifice" rests on the fact that foreign aid represents conscious efforts made by the donor to permit the transfer of resources to recipients. Without such conscious efforts resource transfer would not take place. The donor makes such a "sacrifice," or bears a burden, when it extends part of its resources to recipient countries, either free of charge or at concessional rates. Raymond F. Mikesell, for example, incorporated this concept in his definition of foreign aid which, according to him, is "a transfer of real resources or immediate claim on resources from one country to another, which would not have taken place as a result of the operation of market forces or in the absence of specific official action designed to promote the transfer of the donor country."[5] That this transfer of resources involves sacrifice was indicated by I. M. D. Little and J. M. Clifford, who noted that "there is good reason for supposing that the subsidized transfer of capital or skill, which is properly called aid, is a genuine economic sacrifice."[6] The extent of sacrifice made by Japan in providing aid resources to recipient countries will be examined in Chapter 5. (By determining the changes in the extent of sacrifice made over a period of years, we can ascertain the changes that have taken place in Japanese preferences for certain recipient countries.)

Japanese aid is channeled either directly through bilateral aid arrangements or indirectly through multilateral agencies and programs. The significance of determining the extent to which Japan channels her aid resources bilaterally or multilaterally lies in the extent of control that she can exercise over the actual distribution and utilization of aid funds. Most of the aid funds provided bilaterally had been tied to the procurement of Japanese goods and services until 1972. The extent of multilateral aid provided by Japan indicates both her willingness to contribute to joint international efforts and her readiness to distribute aid funds on rational criteria. (Changes in the nature and extent of Japanese aid provided through multilateral programs will be analyzed in Chapter 7.)

To determine the extent of overall Japanese aid resources and their components in light of the significance attached to them as outlined above, we will examine below the changes over time in Japan's levels of development assistance (ODA), "other" official, flows (OOF) of aid, and private flows of aid in comparison with those of other donors, as reported by DAC and U. N. sources.

Since Japanese foreign aid resources were first provided in the early 1950s, the total flow of Japanese financial aid to less-developed countries increased moderately during the first 15 years and then rapidly during several years since the middle of the 1960s. [7] In 1972 the Japanese government proudly pointed to the fact that the total amount of aid flow from Japan became the second largest donor total, only ranking behind that of the United States; the Japanese total had surpassed that of the United Kingdom in 1968, that of West Germany in 1970, and that of France in 1971. [8] A substantial portion of the total Japanese flow, however, consisted of items that were technically treated as aid resources but could not readily be regarded as such because of their nature or terms. The terms of Japanese loans have gradually eased over the years but continued to remain relatively strict. Less than one-third of the total flow consisted of what might be regarded as genuine aid resources, such as grants, technical assistance, and contributions to multilateral agencies, while more than two-thirds of the total flow represented activities that were of a purely commercial and business nature.

The Japanese government, as noted in Chapter 2, has declared its intention to further expand and improve its aid program. In response to recommendations made by such international bodies as the United Nations Conference on Trade and Development (UNCTAD), DAC, and the Pearson Commission, Japan has pledged not only to provide total foreign aid amounting to 1 percent of her gross national product (GNP) by 1975, but also to raise her level of ODA to 0. 7 percent of her GNP, without indicating specific target date, and to soften her aid terms along the lines of recommendations made over time by DAC. The Japanese government also indicated its intention to expand other aid components, such as grants, technical assistance, multilateral aid contributions, and private investments.

To assess the overall performance of the Japanese aid program, we will first examine Japan's performance in terms of the familiar 1 percent and 0. 7 percent targets. The 1 percent target was first adopted in 1960 by the United Nations General Assembly, which urged the advanced countries to provide one percent of their combined national income for assistance to less-developed countries. Four years later in 1964 UNCTAD proposed that each of the developed countries make available 1 percent of her national income for development assistance. The target was then raised by UNCTAD, at its second session in 1968, to 1 percent of GNP measured at market prices. Concurrently the Pearson Commission strongly recommended in 1969 that each donor take steps to increase her volume of ODA to 0. 7 percent of GNP possibly by 1975 and not later than 1980. The U. N. General Assembly included the Pearson recommendation as

TABLE 3. 1

Total Foreign Aid Flows and Their Percentage of
Gross National Product, 1960-72 (million dollars)

Country	1960	1965	1970	1971	1972	1973
United States	3, 818	5, 445	5, 393	6, 880	7, 574	8, 346
	(0. 75)	(0. 78)	(0. 55)	(0. 66)	(0. 66)	(0. 64)
Japan	246	486	1, 824	2, 141	2, 725	5, 844
	(0. 58)	(0. 55)	(0. 93)	(0. 95)	(0. 93)	(1. 42)
France	1, 325	1, 299	1, 805	1, 624	2, 073	2, 800
	(2. 19)	(1. 30)	(1. 24)	(1. 00)	(1. 06)	(1. 10)
United Kingdom	881	1, 032	1, 238	1, 432	1, 486	1, 058
	(1. 22)	(1. 03)	(1. 02)	(1. 05)	(0. 98)	(0. 61)
Germany	628	724	1, 409	1, 915	1, 714	1, 790
	(0. 88)	(0. 64)	(0. 76)	(0. 88)	(0. 67)	(0. 51)

Note: Percentage of gross national product indicated in paren-
theses.

Source: OECD, Resources for the Developing World, p. 239;
OECD, Development Co-operation: 1971 Review, p. 170; and OECD,
Development Co-operation: 1972 Review, p. 180, and 1974 Review,
pp. 199-200.

part of its international development strategy for the second U. N.
development decade. [9]

In terms of her total flow of financial aid Japan has made substantial progress. The total flow increased gradually from $50 million
in 1955 to $380 million in 1960 and to $490 million by 1965; it then
expanded at an accelerated rate to reach $1, 800 million in 1970,
$2, 100 million in 1971, $2, 700 million by 1972 and $5, 800 million
in 1973. As a result, as shown in Table 3. 1, the share of Japan's
GNP represented by total aid flow increased from about one-half of
one percent in the 1960s to close to one percent by the beginning of
the 1970s. In 1973 total flow represented 1. 42 percent of Japan's
GNP, making the Japanese proud of the accomplishment.[10]

As noted above, Japan's total aid flow includes ODA, OOF, and
private capital flows. ODA consists of development assistance provided by official agencies meeting the following criteria set forth by
DAC: the main objective of the aid is the promotion of the economic
development and welfare of developing countries, and the aid is
concessional in character with its terms significantly softer than the
terms normally available for commercial transactions. [11] As the chairman of DAC, Edwin Martin, declared in 1972, ODA flows are "the only
ones which deserve to be called 'aid' or 'assistance'. "[12] The Pearson
Commission also recognized the significance of ODA; according to the

commission, ODA has become "vital to development planning, as its continuity can be assured and it can be directed to sectors of high priority to the growth process."[13] In practice Japan's ODA has consisted mainly of reparations payments, economic cooperation grants, intergovernmental development loans extended by the Export-Import Bank of Japan and by the Overseas Economic Cooperation Fund (OECF), technical assistance, and contributions to multilateral aid agencies.

Japan's ODA increased steadily from $105 million in 1960 to $244 million in 1965, to $458 million in 1970, $611 million in 1972 and $1,011 million in 1973.[14] As Japan's GNP began to increase rapidly, however, the volume of her ODA as a percentage of her GNP did not show a corresponding increase. ODA represented 0.14 percent of GNP in 1962, increased to 0.27 percent in 1965, and reached a record high of 0.32 percent in 1967. After that ODA declined to 0.23 percent of GNP in 1970 and to 0.21 percent in 1972. Such a downward trend prompted DAC to express its concern in 1972 as to the reliability of the pledge made by the Japanese government to attain the 0.7 percent target in the near future.[15] In response to this and to other international criticism that Japan's ODA was remaining relatively small, the Japanese government attempted to reverse the down trend, with the total amount of Japan's ODA increasing by $400 million, to $1,011 million, in 1973. However, ODA as a percentage of Japan's GNP increased by only 0.04 percent in 1973 to 0.25 percent.[16] As shown in Table 3.2, the ODA share of GNP for Japan remained about 0.10 percent below the average rate for DAC countries as a whole.

In the early years of Japanese aid the terms of official development assistance loans extended by Japan were more strict than the average terms for DAC members as a whole. As will be analyzed in Chapter 5, loans extended by the Export-Import Bank of Japan in the

TABLE 3.2

Official Development Assistance as a Percentage of
Gross National Product, 1962-72

Country	1962	1967	1970	1971	1972	1973
France	1.27	0.71	0.66	0.66	0.67	0.58
Germany	0.45	0.41	0.32	0.34	0.31	0.32
Japan	0.14	0.31	0.23	0.23	0.21	0.25
Sweden	0.12	0.25	0.38	0.44	0.48	0.59
United Kingdom	0.52	0.44	0.37	0.41	0.40	0.35
United States	0.56	0.43	0.31	0.32	0.29	0.23
Total for DAC countries	0.52	0.42	0.34		0.34	0.30

Source: OECD, Development Co-operation: 1973 Review, p. 189.
And 1974 Review, p. 202.

1950s carried the interest rate of 5.76-6.00 percent a year with a maturity period of 10 years and a grace period of 3 years. The terms were gradually softened as the Overseas Economic Cooperation Fund (OECF) began extending easier loans in the early 1960s. By the middle of the 1960s Japanese loans carried a one-half of one percent lower interest rate—5.25-5.50 percent a year—with a maturity period of about 15 years and a grace period of 5 years. During the next several years the Japanese government made further efforts to ease terms; by the beginning of the 1970s the average interest rate went down to about 3.5 percent a year with an average maturity period of 20 years and an average grace period of 6-7 years. Yet this softening of Japanese loan terms was not sufficient either to meet the average terms of loans extended by other DAC members or to fulfill any of the DAC recommendations made on aid loan terms. [17]

In 1971 a standard Japanese loan carried an annual interest rate of 3.5 percent and a maturity period of 22.1 years, with a grace period of 6.7 years, as shown in Table 3.3. In the following two years the terms eased a bit, but not much. As a result they were still stricter than the terms recommended by the Pearson Commission, a 2 percent annual interest rate with a maturity period of between 25 and 40 years including a grace period of 7 to 10 years. [18]

The overall rather poor accomplishments of Japan in her efforts to fulfill the targets set forth by various international bodies is due not only to the hard terms of her aid loans but to relatively small shares in her aid program of such genuine aid items as grants, technical assistance, and contributions to multilateral aid agencies. Together these items accounted for only about 10 percent of total Japanese aid in 1972 and they were still less in financial value than comparable aid extended by the United Kingdom, West Germany, and France, although Japan's total flow of financial resources to less-developed countries and multilateral institutions was larger than that of these other nations. [19]

Until the late 1960s Japanese grants consisted mainly of the baisho payments and economic cooperation grants. The baisho payments were made to four Southeast Asian countries—Burma, Indonesia, the Philippines, and South Vietnam—and amounted to a little more than $1 billion in total. Economic cooperation grants were extended to eight Asian countries—Burma, Cambodia, Laos, the Federation of Malaysia, Singapore, South Korea, South Vietnam, and Thailand. The total value of these grants amounted to about $500 million. The significance of both the baisho and economic cooperation grants lies, first, in the fact that they represented, directly or indirectly, settlements from World War II. And, second, in their forming of the major portion of the entire grant component of Japanese aid (see Chapter 4).

Japan's technical assistance activities have remained minor and smaller in scale compared to those of any other major donors in spite of the claim by the Japanese government that Japan is exceptionally

28

TABLE 3.3

Terms of Official Development Assistance Loans, 1971 and 1972

Country	ODA Commitments ($ million)			Maturity (years)			Interest Rate (percent)			Grace Period (years)		
	1971	1972	1973	1971	1972	1973	1971	1972	1973	1971	1972	1973
France	1,309.8	1,802.8	1,790.9	17.7	15.3	21.6	4.0	4.1	3.4	2.4	3.2	4.6
Germany	950.7	1,126.5	1,605.6	29.6	28.9	30.8	2.0	2.6	2.2	6.6	8.3	9.1
Japan	769.8	1,018.7	1,364.5	22.1	21.2	24.6	3.5	3.9	3.7	6.7	6.4	7.7
Sweden	199.7	253.2	406.1	48.6	46.0	47.1	0.8	0.9	0.9	10.0	10.0	10.0
United Kingdom	713.7	900.2	774.0	24.1	22.5	24.9	1.6	1.4	1.1	6.2	5.9	6.1
United States	3,911.8	4,504.3	4,396.1	35.7	37.1	40.1	2.9	2.6	2.6	8.7	9.7	10.7

Source: OECD, Development Co-operation: 1973 Review, p. 48. And 1974 Review, p. 236.

TABLE 3. 4

Technical Cooperation, 1967-1973

	Amount ($million)	Students and Trainees Received	Experts and Volunteers Supplied
France			
1967	403	16, 263	46, 363
1970	438	14, 191	38, 122
1973	685	14, 599	34, 033
Germany			
1967	115	14, 767	5, 622
1970	190	19, 646	6, 344
1973	299	24, 242	7, 117
Japan			
1967	11	1, 701	1, 247
1970	22	3, 675	2, 629
1973	57	5, 743	3, 497
United Kingdom			
1967	92	9, 490	18, 854
1970	109	12, 056	17, 354
1973	178	15, 002	14, 688
United States			
1967	564	19, 242	29, 952
1970	578	18, 272	22, 417
1973	613	14, 628	12, 119

Source: OECD, Development Co-operation: 1974 Review, pp. 289-91.

suited to offer her technical know-how. While the total cost of Japanese technical assistance increased by six times between 1960 and 1970, it amounted to only 1. 2 percent of Japan's total aid flow and 4. 7 percent of her ODA in 1970. [20] Even in 1973, as shown in Table 3. 4, the cost of Japanese technical assistance was less than one-tenth of the cost of technical assistance provided either by the United States or France and about one-seventh of that of West Germany and one-third of that of the United Kingdom. Such comparisons of course should not be made solely on monetary grounds since the cost of technical advisory services and the personnel supplied differ substantially from one country to another. Comparisons should instead be made in terms of the actual numbers of technical experts and volunteers sent by donor countries to developing nations and the numbers of students and trainees received by donors from developing nations. Compared against such criteria, the difference between Japan and other donor countries becomes smaller, but it is still considerable. The number of technical personnel sent by Japan was only 3, 500 in 1973, representing about one-tenth of the number of technical personnel sent by France and about half the number sent by West Germany. The number of students and trainees received by Japan was about one-third of those received by France, the United Kingdom and the United States and one-fourth of the number received by Germany.

Like her technical assistance, Japan's participation in, and contributions to, multilateral aid agencies and programs started developing in the early 1950s and remained modest until the middle of the 1960s. After that, however, Japan's multilateral contributions expanded substantially. The total value of Japan's multilateral ODA, that is, contributions, capital subscriptions, and concessional loans provided to multilateral institutions, was less than $10 million until the mid-1960s, but increased to $45 million by 1967. Three years later it almost doubled to $87 million, in 1970 and then multiplied rapidly. In 1973 it amounted to $246 million (see Table 3. 5). (Chapter 7 will describe how Japan's multilateral aid has grown over the postwar years and particularly since the middle of the 1960s.)

Regarding the magnitude of the other components of Japanese aid—the so-called other official flows (OOF) and private capital flows—the link between the two flows indicates how closely official aid resources are directed for the encouragement of private activities in less-developed countries. OOF consist of official export credits, equity investment credits and capital subscriptions, and purchases of bonds issued by multilateral aid agencies at close to market terms. These flows are often provided to supplement the financial requirements

TABLE 3. 5

Official Development Assistance Contributions to
Multilateral Agencies, 1964-1973 ($ million)

	1964	1967	1970	1973
Canada	16. 4	46. 2	78. 6	165. 5
Denmark	7. 9	13. 4	21. 7	59. 9
France	17. 8	49. 9	102. 9	194. 1
Germany	24. 6	72. 4	132. 9	310. 6
Italy	4. 6	31. 3	84. 5	73. 8
Japan	9. 6	44. 7	86. 5	245. 8
Netherlands	16. 2	39. 7	41. 8	92. 1
Sweden	19. 1	33. 8	53. 9	122. 2
United Kingdom	45. 7	53. 1	47. 9	160. 8
United States	222. 5	306. 6	393. 0	631. 0

Source: OECD, Development Co-operation: 1974 Review, p. 254.

TABLE 3.6

Net Other Official Aid Flows, 1970 and 1972 (million dollars)

Country	1970	1971	1972	1973
Japan	693.6	651.1	856.4	1,178.9
United States	168.0	180.0	196.0	477.0
Italy	29.5	121.6	148.6	343.8
Germany	132.1	164.2	148.5	229.2
Canada	56.5	66.1	114.1	76.1
France	28.0	50.2	16.5	77.4
United Kingdom	6.5	12.0	16.3	40.7

Source: OECD, Development Co-operation: 1972 Review, pp. 218-19, Development Co-operation: 1973 Review, pp. 186-87; 1974 Review, pp. 212-15.

of transactions attempted by private groups and multilateral institutions. Private flows represent transactions financed by private groups to provide both export and import credits and capital needed for direct and portfolio investments. Since private flows are aimed at carrying out purely commercial and business activities, they may not necessarily be considered as aid resources. DAC, for example, in 1972 stopped considering OOF and private flows as actual development assistance, although both figures are still added up as part of the total financial flows to less-developed countries and multilateral institutions. [21]

Since many aid transactions consist of both official and private capital, it is sometimes difficult to determine the exact composition of any particular aid loans and credits made available jointly by official or private sources. Export and import credits are often extended by such private sources as regular commercial banks.

The net total of Japan's OOF changed little until the middle of the 1960s. In fact the net amount actually decreased from $114 million in 1961 to $110 million in 1965 after $76 million was deducted for amortization. In the following five years, however, the net amount of OOF increased by six times and totaled $694 million in 1970. In 1972 it reached $856 million, and in 1973 it increased by a further $220 million to $1,179 million. Consequently Japan's OOF became became by far the largest among all of the donors including the United States (see Table 3.6).

The growth pattern of Japan's OOF and her private flows illustrates the close complementing of official aid resources and private trade and investment funds. As will be analyzed in Chapter 5, both the Export-Import Bank of Japan and OECF extend loan funds to private Japanese business firms. These loans usually constitute part of the

TABLE 3.7

Net Flow of Private Capital, 1963-73 (million dollars)

Year	France	Italy	Germany	Japan	UK	USA
1963	391.3	242.6	185.9	93.9	306.3	880.0
1964	504.2	196.6	283.5	79.1	425.5	1,879.7
1965	514.2	172.5	263.6	132.1	547.1	1,859.0
1966	553.6	516.6	302.6	159.1	398.0	1,505.5
1967	498.5	131.4	598.6	214.3	326.0	2,089.7
1968	846.4	400.9	1,068.3	390.5	407.4	2,486.6
1969	751.3	710.5	1,500.7	451.7	707.7	1,568.0
1970	835.6	505.2	756.0	672.3	774.2	2,992.7
1971	498.0	566.6	1,016.8	978.7	858.0	3,384.0
1972	740.1	440.2	799.4	1,257.9	883.2	4,029.0
1973	1,234.3	109.2	458.8	3,654.3	414.4	4,901.0

Source: OECD, Development Co-operation: 1974 Review, p. 205.

33

entire aid and investment programs in which regular commercial banks also participate. The rapid increase in the flow of Japan's OOF was paralleled by an equally rapid increase in Japanese export and investment activities in less-developed countries. The volume of guaranteed private export credits was less than $50 million in the early 1960s. As a result of Japan's economic expansion abroad since the middle of the 1960s, net private capital flows from Japan to less-developed countries increased rapidly after 1965, compared to earlier variances from one year to the next without tangible move in any direction (see Table 3.7). In 1971 net private flows from Japan amounted to close to $1 billion, and in the following year they increased by more than 25 percent. However, the 1972 Japanese figure was still about one-third of the private capital extended by the United States — $3,380 million, although Japan's figure was already larger than comparable figures for any other countries except Germany. Japan's private flows then almost tripled in reaching $3,654 million, making Japan second only to the United States. Most of the increase resulted from an enormous gain in direct Japanese investment, which alone climbed from $844 million in 1972 to $3,072 million in 1973.[22] As will be analyzed in Chapter 6, an increasing amount of private funds, together with OOF funds, went to countries with rich natural and energy resources. The heavy concentration of Japanese financial resources in these countries, however, in 1974 caused alarm among some of the DAC members assessing Japanese aid performance. These nations pointed out that Japanese aid resources were unduly concentrated in countries that needed foreign aid most.[23] Whether or not certain countries such as those with rich natural resources have in fact been favored by Japan in her aid program will be discussed in Chapters 5 and 6.

NOTES

1. Sangyo Kongyo Kozo Shingi Kai Kokusai Keizaibu Kai, Nippon no Taigai Seisaku (Tokyo: Daiyamendo Sha, 1972), pp. 4, 126-150. The major policy recommendations on Japanese overseas economic cooperation, for example, were made by the Industrial Structure Deliberation Council (Sangyo Kozo Singikai) in 1972. The Council consisted of business leaders, university professors, researchers and press. The Committee on International Economy, which drafted the recommendations, had a total membership of 34.
2. Robert S. Ozaki, "Japan's Role in Asian Economic Development," Asian Survey 7, no. 4, April 1967; pp. 237-44.
3. OECD, Resources for the Developing World: the Flow of Financial Resources to Less-Developed Countries, 1962-1968 (Paris, 1970), p. 317. The term "financial resources" is used by DAC to

refer to the value of goods and services as well as purchasing power transferred.

4. J. Stephen Hoadley and Sukehiro Hasegawa, "Sino-Japanese Relations, 1950-1970: An Application of the Linkage Model of the International Politics," International Studies Quarterly, June 1971, pp. 131-157.

5. Raymond F. Mikesell, The Economics of Foreign Aid (Chicago: Aldine, 1968), p. 194.

6. I. M. D. Little and J. M. Clifford, International Aid (Chicago: Aldine Publishing Co., 1965), p. 81.

7. See OECD, Development Assistance; 1969 Review (Paris, 1970), annex I and OECD, Resources for the Developing World: the Flow of Financial Resources to Less Developed Countries, 1962-1968 (Paris, 1970), annex III for discussion of the magnitude of the total flow and its composition.

8. Tsusansho, Keizai Kyoryoku no Genjo to Mondai-ten: 1972 (Tokyo: 1972), pp. 92-94.

9. Lester S. Pearson et al., Partners in Development (New York: Praeger, 1968), pp. 148-49 and General Assembly resolution 2626 (XXV), paragraph 42, of October 24, 1970, General Assembly Official Records: Twenty-fifth Session, supplement no. 28 (A/8028).

10. Kokusai Kaihatsu Janaru 8, no. 11 (Tokyo: July 10, 1974), pp. 48-49.

11. See OECD, Development Co-operation; 1973 Review (Paris, 1973), p. 40. Grant element of 25 percent has been chosen by DAC as a condition for meeting concessionality of development loans.

12. OECD, Development Co-operation; 1972 Review (Paris, 1972), p. 11.

13. Pearson et al., Partners in Development op. cit., p. 148.

14. OECD, Development Co-operation: 1972 Review, p. 170 and 1973 p. 188, and 1974 Review, p. 201.

15. Ibid., p. 46.

16. OECD, Development Co-operation; 1974 Review, p. 202.

17. See OECD, Development Co-operation; 1972 Review (Paris, 1972), pp. 58-59. Under the 1965 DAC recommendations, a country was deemed to have possessed the requirements if one of three conditions were met: (1) at least 81 percent of the total commitments were grants and loans at 3 percent interest or less; (2) 82 percent of the commitments were grants and loans with a maturity of 25 years or more; or (3) a weighted average of grace period of loans was 6.4 years or less. See OECD, Development Assistance; 1970 Review, (Paris, 1970), pp. 46-48. Under the 1969 recommendations, three alternative approaches suggested were the grant test, the minimum concessional element test, and the average concessional element test. Under the grant test, at least 70 percent of ODA commitments must be grants. Countries that passed this test in 1972 were Australia, Austria, Belgium, Denmark, France, Norway and Sweden.

Under the minimum concessional element test, at least 85 percent of ODA has a minimum grant element of 61 percent each. Countries that did not pass the first test but passed this test were Canada, West Germany, Switzerland, the United Kingdom, and the United States. Under the average concessional element test, 85 percent of ODA must contain an average grant element of at least 85 percent. In addition to those countries that passed the first and second tests, the Netherlands passed the third test. Japan, Italy, and Portugal did not pass any of the three tests.

18. Pearson et al., Partners in Development, op. cit., p. 164.

19. OECD, Development Co-operation: 1973 Review (Paris: 1973), pp. 186-87.

20. Kaigai Gijutsu Kyoryoku Jigyodan, Gijutsu Kyoryoku Nempo: 1971 (Tokyo: 1970), p. 11.

21. OECD, Development Co-operation: 1972 Review (Paris: 1972), p. 11.

22. Kokusai Kaihatsu Janarau 8, no. 11 (July 10, 1974), pp. 48-49.

23. Asahi Shimbun, July 20, 1974.

4

SIGNIFICANCE OF
BAISHO AND ECONOMIC
COOPERATION GRANTS

The baisho, or reparations, payments were made by the Japanese government to countries whose former territories were occupied or damaged by Japanese military forces before and during World War II. What countries received the baisho payments, and the magnitude and contents of the baisho, depended largely on the priorities accorded to them by the Japanese government in terms of Japan's national political and economic goals. (As noted in Chapter 3, the baisho were accepted by the Development Assistance Committee of the Organization for Economic Cooperation and Development (OECD) as part of Japan's aid to less-developed countries, although inclusion of the baisho as aid may be questioned on the basis of circumstances that compelled Japan to make the payments.) In addition to the baisho a number of economic cooperation grants, as noted previously, were provided by Japan to several Asian countries that abandoned their claims for the baisho. These grants are sometimes called reparation-like payments since they were extended in lieu of the baisho. This chapter will describe not only the circumstances that led Japan to make the baisho and related payments, but the objectives Japan sought to attain through these payments, how the recipients and levels of payments were decided, and their overall effects on the Japanese economy.

Following her defeat in World War II, Japan set as her immediate national goals (1) protection from external aggression; (2) rehabilitation from the devastation of the war; and (3) reentry into kokusai shakai, or the international community. The Japanese government was then convinced that the first goal could be reached only through U.S. military protection and the second goal through hard work on the part of the Japanese people. The third goal was expected to be attained through the normalization of diplomatic relations with European and North American countries and the establishment of diplomatic ties with neighboring nations by settling various issues that had arisen out of the war. Reparations and reparation-like payments were made prerequisites by some Southeast Asian countries for the conclusion of their peace treaties with Japan.

At the beginning of the 1950s, as Edwin O. Reischauer noted, the United States had three alternative courses to take in her future handling of Japan: the first option was to continue military occupation indefinitely, the second was to grant Japan quasi-independence, and the third was to restore full sovereignty to Japan by negotiating a peace treaty with or without Communist participation. [1] Since the United States decided on the negotiation of a peace treaty with Japan, the Japanese government became eager to sign the treaty, even if Japan had to make substantial concessions to the Allied powers. Thus Japan accepted an obligation to make reparation payments, provided that the exact level of payments could be decided realistically. The baisho provision was then included in Article 14 of the San Francisco treaty (signed in 1951), compelling Japan to pay reparations to the Allied countries for the damages and suffering inflicted on these countries during the war. The article specifically stated:

> Japan will promptly enter into negotiations with Allied
> Powers so desiring, whose present territories were
> occupied by Japanese forces and damaged by Japan, with
> a view to assisting to compensate those countries for the
> cost of repairing the damage done, by making available the
> services of the Japanese people in production, salvaging
> and other work for the Allied Powers in question. Such
> arrangements shall avoid the imposition of additional
> liabilities on other Allied Powers, and, where the Manu-
> facturing of raw materials is called for, they shall be
> supplied by the Allied Powers in question, so as not to
> throw any foreign exchange burden upon Japan. [2]

With Japan's signing of the San Francisco peace treaty, the reparations payments became legal requirements as laid down in the treaty; but legality was not the only reason Japan agreed to the arrangement. Politically Japan agreed to pay reparations because of both her desire to return to the International community as soon as possible and her ideological commitment at that time to anti-communism. Economically the baisho were used (1) to assist in the recovery of the Japanese economy, (2) to promote exports of Japanese goods, and (3) to facilitate heavy industrialization at home.

POLITICAL AND DIPLOMATIC OBJECTIVES

As noted above, national security, reconstruction, and reentry into the international community were the major political and diplomatic goals of Japan during the years immediately following her recovery of sovereignty in 1952. The United States and Western European countries posed little difficulty for the normalization of their diplomatic ties with Japan; as East-West confrontations mounted these nations were eager to strengthen their ties with Japan and solidify their anti-Communist network. To the United States and Western Europe the problem of Germany was more pertinent and pressing than that of Japan during World War II and in the immediate postwar era.

To Southeast Asians, however, Japan's emergence as a world power within a short period of time after the Meiji restoration carried profound implications. Asians viewed Japan as the only Asian country that had successfully acquired modern technology and become a power in economic and military strength. Many of the Asian leaders regarded Japan as a prime example to follow, although Japan's actions preceding and during World War II had had negative as well as positive effects. While Japanese forces had expelled Western colonial rulers from Asia, they had also exploited their fellow Asians. As Yoshiyuki Hagiwara pointed out: "On the one hand, it terminated European colonialism in Asia, paving the way for independence in these countries. On the other hand, the extremely cruel and oppressive treatment at the hands of the Japanese army whipped up popular outrage and strong anti-Japanese movements."[3]

Thus Japan had been both a liberator and a new colonial exploiter, and the response of Southeast Asians to Japanese military occupation was a mixture of appreciation and outrage. Those countries that strongly appreciated the "liberation" aspect of Japan's actions were ready to embark on a new diplomatic relationship with Japan once the war ended, while those countries that most resented Japan's neocolonialism were determined to get from her as much compensation as possible before establishing diplomatic ties with her. Adverse feeling toward Japan reached its peak among the people of Korea and the Philippines, while both the Taiwanese and Burmese maintained a comparatively lenient attitude toward Japan.

With the Communist governments refusing to sign the San Francisco peace treaty, it became clear to the Japanese as to what nations were to be the bargaining governments in reparations negotiations. Thus during the following twenty years Japan conducted such negotiations with most of the East and Southeast Asian countries; the Communist countries were, at least initially, automatically excluded from the list of countries with which any possible negotiations could take place.

A total of ten countries accepted either reparations (baisho) or reparation-like payments from Japan, while the Chinese (both People's Republic of China and the Republic of China) abandoned their claim for reparations. The breakdown of recipients and nonrecipients of payments is given in the following lists:

Recipients of Reparations (Baisho) Payments

Burma
Indonesia
Philippines
Republic of Vietnam (South Vietnam)

Recipients of Reparation-like (Economic Cooperation) Grants

Burma	Republic of Korea (South Korea)
Cambodia	Republic of Vietnam (South Vietnam)
Laos	Singapore
Malaysia	Thailand

Nonrecipients

People's Republic of China (Mainland China)
Republic of China (Taiwan)
Democratic People's Republic of Korea (North Korea)
Democratic Republic of Vietnam (North Vietnam)

Two of these countries, the Philippines and South Vietnam, formally demanded reparations payments according to Article 14 of the San Francisco peace treaty, and signed their agreements with Japan in 1956 and 1959, respectively. Indonesia signed the San Francisco peace treaty but did not ratify it. Subsequently a separate peace treaty and a reparations payment agreement were negotiated between Japan and Indonesia; these were signed in 1958. Burma did not participate in the San Francisco peace conference but undertook her own baisho negotiations with Japan expeditiously, becoming (in 1954) the first country to sign a reparations agreement with Japan. The Republic of China (Taiwan) and the People's Republic of China (Mainland China) did not press for reparations payments. The Nationalist Chinese instead found it politically advantageous to gain Japanese recognition of their regime as the sole representative government of China. By the time a normalization of diplomatic relations between Peking and Tokyo was achieved, in 1972, the Communist Chinese were content with an indication of Japan's regret for what the Japanese had done in China during World War II. Both Chinese governments considered it almost an act of revenge to demand reparations. Cambodia and Laos disclaimed reparations payments as such, but asked for economic and technical assistance in the form of grants. Since Japan also preferred this approach, she negotiated similar grant arrangements with Malaysia, Singapore, and South Korea. Japan furthermore agreed to compensate for economic damages incurred in Thailand as a result of the issuing of yen during the war. [4]

The most significant aspect of the baisho settlement is the fact that Japan had no hesitation in undertaking and, concluding the baisho negotiations with the governments of Nationalist China, South Vietnam, and South Korea; the (Japanese) readiness to negotiate with these governments which represented only one side of the divided countries indicated thinking and attitudes of the current Japanese leaders, who formulated their foreign policies within a framework set up by the United States in the era of East-West confrontation. Japan sided with countries in the Western camp, led by the United States, and extended material aid to those countries confronting the Communist camp, led by the Soviet Union.

The main objective of Japanese leaders at the time, particularly those in the Ministry of Foreign Affairs (Gaimusho), was to sign agreements with Southeast Asian countries that were in the non-Communist bloc. Reflecting such a view, Gaimusho reported in 1963 that the baisho negotiations had been fully completed when the second round of negotiations with Burma was concluded in March 1963.[5]

China and Korea both posed particularly difficult and lengthy negotiating problems for the Japanese. Part of China (Taiwan) and all of Korea had been colonies of Japan respectively since 1895 and 1906, but both countries were now divided and ruled under two opposing regimes.

The normalization of diplomatic relations between Japan and South Korea required 15 years of hard negotiations and created domestic turmoil in both countries. While both countries were within the orbit of American military protection after World War II, they were wide apart in their sentiment toward each other. Korean dislike of the Japanese was matched only by strong Japanese antipathy toward Koreans. Bitter memories of harsh Japanese colonial rule made it difficult for the Koreans to accept an easy settlement with the Japanese. The government of Syngman Rhee, generally expressing the feeling of most South Koreans, took a hard line in its dealings with Japan. When negotiations between the two countries first started in 1951, the Rhee government demanded $800 million in reparations, along with other claims. These claims were listed as eight separate demands:[6] (1) the immediate return of Korean national treasures and historical items reportedly taken out of Korea by the Japanese during the colonial period; (2) the immediate return of gold and silver also reportedly taken out of Korea by the Japanese; (3) the immediate return of original Korean maps and documents; (4) payments for those Koreans who died during Japanese military campaigns and for Korean laborers who were unduly exploited by the Japanese during the Second World War; (5) a settlement for the Japanese yen issued in Korea during the war; (6) a settlement on Japanese securities and bonds held by Koreans; (7) the return of property belonging to the labor union of the colonial railroad in Korea; and (8) the return of property held by a Korean scholarship foundation in Japan.

In addition to these claims a number of other issues contributed to the difficulty of achieving rapprochement between the two countries.

41

These issues included the legal status of 750,000 Koreans residing in Japan, the territorial conflict involving Takeshima and adjacent islands, and fishing rights within the Rhee border. As a result little progress was made in the Japanese-Korean normalization process during the 1950s.

A change in leadership in South Korea in 1960 and 1961 brought about a turn in the negotiations, with the Korean government now more willing to settle outstanding differences over compensation for the period of Japanese rule and for territorial claims. Yet both the Japanese and South Korean governments were accused by their respective opposition political parties of making unnecessary concessions simply to normalize relations between the two countries. The Ikeda government was hesitant to confront its opposition party and wanted to avoid a recurrence of the national crisis that had toppled the Kishi government in 1960 following the renewal of the U.S.-Japan security treaty. The Park government in South Korea was also cautious during its initial years in power so as not to antagonize domestic forces bitterly opposed to Japan. It was not until 1965 that the Japanese government headed by Sato concluded a peace treaty with Korea and settled the issue of compensation for damage done by the Japanese in Korea before and during the Second World War.

According to the agreement Japan was to provide South Korea with $300 million in Japanese goods and services within a period of ten years. This payment was to be made at an annual rate of $30 million. In addition the Overseas Economic Cooperation Fund was to extend $200 million in credits to Korea at an interest rate of 3.5 percent for a maturity period of 20 years including a grace period of 7 years.

The case of China was an equally slow and difficult settlement for Japan to make, but also revealed a basic difference in the relationship between the Chinese and Japanese in contrast to dealings between the Koreans and Japanese. The Chinese and Japanese have for many years held a certain respect for each other. Japan has borrowed extensively from China in the cultural sphere, while the Chinese have admired the Japanese for their technological and economic advancement.

In signing a peace treaty with Nationalist China, Japan at first hoped to leave the door open for normalizing her ties with Communist China; the Yoshida government noted in a protocol accompanying the peace treaty that the treaty applied only to territories covered by Nationalist control. While Yoshida and his successors had no illusion about Communist control over the Chinese mainland, they were convinced that Japan's security would not be assured in this case without American presence in Japan. To secure such military presence throughout the postwar era, the Japanese government sided with the United States on almost all of the international issues of the period, including the China question.

The Japanese nonetheless maintained unofficial ties with Mainland China through such subnational links as trade and cultural exchanges. With a small number of barter transactions conducted in the early 1950s, trade between the two countries increased gradually under the cover of "friendly trade" and "Liao-Takasaki" agreements. Japan's trade with China remained relatively small due to export limitations imposed by the China Committee of the Consultative Group (CHINCOM), which was formed in 1952. Japanese exports to China never exceeded 3 percent of total Japanese exports in the 1960s. As the renewal of the U. S. -Japanese security treaty became a major political issue in the late 1950s, trade between Japan and China began to decline; the downfall of the Kishi government and the advent of the Ikeda government then were followed by an expansion of trade. The principle of sekei-bunri, or a separation of politics and economics, was devised by the Ikeda government, and adopted by the Sato government, to avoid the issue of the two Chinas. However, Japan had no way of ignoring indefinitely this central problem in her relationship with China.

Following the establishment of rapprochement between the United States and the People's Republic of China in 1972, Japan promptly entered into negotiations to normalize her own diplomatic relations with the People's Republic of China. Unlike most, however, the Chinese demanded no reparations payments, but asked that the Japanese merely apologize for suffering dealt to the Chinese people during the war. The communique signed at the conclusion negotiations by Chou En-lai and Kakuei Tanaka noted the Japanese prime minister's "regret, " but had no provision for baisho payments. [7]

Three sets of factors seemed to have led the Chinese not to demand payments: geopolitical, economic, and cultural-psychological. First, the governments in both Peking and Taipei hoped, through establishing diplomatic and economic ties with Japan, to strengthen their respective positions in claiming sovereignty over all of China. Being one of the major powers in Asia, Japan's recognition carried significant weight. Second, reparations payments were considered minor by the Chinese in comparison with the potential benefits that commercial ties with Japan could bring; the scope of trade and invest-ment was expected to grow so wide that next to this reparations pay-ments would seem relatively trivial. Third, and most important, as Aikhiro Kasai pointed out, the Chinese considered any claim for reparations payments to be an act of vengeance that they wished to avoid: after all, not only Japan but other imperialist countries had attempted to cut a slice of the Chinese pie in the past. [8]

Determination of Size of Payments

As indicated above, the basic decisions to pay reparations were made by the Japanese for political and diplomatic reasons. Once such a decision was made, the Japanese made sure, through both lengthy negotiations and administrative measures, that their own economic interests were protected and advanced. Japanese representatives sat at the negotiating tables in tough, businesslike fashion; Lawrence Olson's account of the bargaining sessions noted this firm, almost ruthless, attitude of the Japanese negotiators:

> The Japanese accepted the obligation to pay what was
> imposed upon them by the peace settlement. . . . How-
> ever, reparations, like all transactions involving the
> transfer of resources, were regarded by the Japanese as an
> occasion for the most dogged bargaining, unclouded by the
> influence of any sentimental regard for the recipients in
> whatever country. [9]

Economically, in undertaking the reparations payments the Japanese aimed at (1) holding the total amount of payments within the paying capacity of the Japanese economy, (2) minimizing any adverse effects on both the Japanese balance of trade and balance of payments, (3) opening up and expanding her markets in Southeast Asia, and (4) facilitating the recovery and expansion of the Japanese economy as a whole.

Throughout the negotiations the Japanese sought to ensure that the size of their payments remained at a reasonable level and within the paying capacity of the economy. In expressing this economic concern they reiterated what Article 14 of the San Francisco peace treaty had stated: "the resources of Japan are not presently sufficient, if it is to maintain a viable economy, to make complete reparation for all such damage and suffering and at the same time meet its other obligations." [10]

Among the four countries that claimed reparations, Indonesia and the Philippines demanded payments far larger than Japan could possibly consider, but Burma made what appeared to the Japanese to be a more reasonable request. Negotiations between Burma and Japan lasted only a few months, and thus the first Japanese reparations agreement was signed in 1954. Initially the Burmese claimed more than $1 billion, but the Japanese offered less than $100 million. Following the bargaining they agreed on an amount of $200 million to be paid to Burma over 10 years. In addition the Japanese agreed to extend $50 million in private loans to Burma and to reexamine the agreement if other countries later received more than the amount received by Burma.

The Indonesian delegation initially demanded $18 billion in consumer goods and services in 1951, and the Philippines, following up Indonesia's claim within a few months, asked for $8 billion in cash (these claims totaled more than the entire gross national product of Japan at that time). The Japanese reacted to the magnitude of the Indonesian claim simply by not acting on it for almost a year following the start of meetings between the two countries. In December 1952 Japan responded to the Philippine demand with a list of services that she would provide to the Philippines as stipulated under Articla 14 of the San Francisco treaty. The list included such activities as the salvaging of sunken ships, the providing of new vessels, and the providing of farm and mining machinery, among other equipment; the Japanese indicated the amount involved in these services was $200 million. In the spring of 1954 Japanese and Philippine negotiators drew up a preliminary overall agreement. This agreement called for Japanese investments, amounting to $400 million over ten years, for the development of natural resources in Mindanao and Luzon. The Japanese were also to assist in the reclamation of land in Mindanao for growing rice that could be exported to Japan. However, due to numerous differences of opinion between Japanese and Philippine diplomats on the adequacy of the exact amount of the settlement, negotiations dragged on until the two countries reached an agreement in April 1956: Japan agreed to provide $500 million in reparations goods over 20 years, $30 million in technical services, and $20 million in cash for Filipino war widows and orphans. In addition the Japanese government promised it would induce $250 million in private loans and credits to the Philippines.

Following this settlement both Indonesia and South Vietnam settled their reparations claims respectively in 1958 and 1959. Japan agreed on reparations for Indonesia totaling $223 million to be paid over a period of 12 years plus $400 million in private loans and investments. Moreover the Japanese agreed to cancel the Indonesian trade deficit amounting at that time to $177 million. Meanwhile South Vietnam was to get $39 million for the construction of a hydroelectric dam over the Da Ninh River. [11] This meant that Japan had agreed to pay a total of $1,012 million to the four reparations-seeking countries (see Table 4.1).

To those other countries in East and Southeast Asia that did not specifically claim reparations in terms of the provisions of the San Francisco treaty Japan, as noted previously, agreed to extend economic cooperation grants, or reparation-like payments; these grants went to Burma, the Khmer Republic (Cambodia), Laos, South Korea, Malaysia, and Singapore. Burma had earlier received reparations under the treaty but demanded that Japan pay her an additional sum in view of the large payments made to both Indonesia and the Philippines. As a result Japan agreed to pay Burma an additional $140 million as economic and technical cooperation grants. Japan also pledged $4.17 million

TABLE 4.1

Japanese Reparations Payments

Recipient Country	Total Payment ($ million)	Annual Payment ($ million)	Period of Payment (years)
Burma	200	20	April 1955-65
Philippines	550	{25 (first 10 years), 30 (second 10 years)	July 1957-76
Indonesia	223	{20 (first 11 years), 3 (12th year)	April 1958-70
South Vietnam	39	{10 (first 3 years), 4.5 (last 2 years)	January 1960-65
Total	1,012		

Source: Gaimusho, Keizai Kyoryoku no Genjo to Mondai-ten (1967), p. 82.

and $2.78 million in cooperation grants respectively to the Khmer Republic and Laos. In the case of Thailand, Japan promised to pay $26.67 million as a "special yen settlement" to compensate for the issuance of yen in Thailand during the war. The economic and technical cooperation grants totaled $489.96 million, as shown in Table 4.2.

Effects on Japanese Economy

The effects of both reparations and reparation-like payments turned out to be encouraging, rather than damaging, for the rehabilitation of the Japanese economy. Not only did payments constitute only one fifth of 1 percent of Japan's gross national product (GNP) throughout the payment period, but by providing industrial goods through the payments Japan opened up export markets in the recipient countries.

As shown in Table 4.3 the payments have been fairly evenly distributed over each payment year, averaging about $70 million. Moreover as the Japanese economy expanded in the 1960s, the payments took a steadily smaller share of GNP. By the mid-1960s few people in Japan were concerned that the payments might burden the economy.

The extent of the burden placed by reparation and reparation-like payments on Japan's national budget has likewise been small: it has averaged 1.5 percent of the annual general national budget. In 1956 the payments were 0.6 percent of the budget, and they increased to

1. 1 percent in both 1957 and 1958. They reached a record high of 2. 1 percent in 1959, when payments to South Vietnam were started, and then declined to the 1. 5 percent average in 1960.

The percentage of payments in the general budget was about the same as the percentage of payments in the budget for science and technology development but well below the share in both the unemployment and social security budgets. Moreover it was larger than the percentage in the budgets for housing, educational assistance, and medium and small industry. [12]

Meanwhile the baisho seemed to contribute to the postwar recovery and expansion of the Japanese economy, first by constituting a stimulus to the economy, which reached its prewar level by the middle of the 1950s, and then by becoming an instrument for some industries and firms to expand their production for export.

As Alan H. Gleason calculated, the estimated real GNP per capita in Japan reached its average prewar level by 1955: The reparation payments, leading to the procurement of goods produced by private industries and firms, stimulated production. Partly due to this increased demand created by the baisho, the Japanese economy continued to grow and its GNP per capita rose rapidly starting in the late 1950s, as shown in Table 4. 4.

During the early period of reparations negotiations, Japan pointed out to the prospective recipients that it was ready to provide only services of Japanese experts and technicians as stipulated under the San Francisco peace treaty. Any provision of goods, the Japanese noted, would burden Japan's fragile balance of payments. The claiming

TABLE 4. 2

Japanese Economic and Technical Cooperation Grants

Recipient Country	Total Amount ($ million)	Annual Amount ($ million)	Period of Payments (years)
Burma	140. 0	11. 7[a]	April 1965-77
South Korea	300. 0	30. 0	December 1965-75
Malaysia	8. 17	Equally divided	May 1968-72
Singapore	8. 17	Equally divided	May 1968-72
Thailand[b]	26. 67	2. 87 (first 7 years)	May 1962-70
Laos	2. 78	1. 39	January 1959-61
Cambodia	4. 17	1. 39	January 1959-61
Total	489. 96		

[a] 11. 3 million for 12th year.
[b] Regarded as "special yen settlement."
Source: Nihon Keizai Shinbun Sha, Nanboku Mondai Nyumon (Tokyo: Nippon Keizai Shinbun Sha, 1971), p. 221.

47

TABLE 4.3

Japanese Reparations Measured Against Japan's Gross National Product

Year	Reparations ($ million)	GNP ($ billion)	Reparations as Percent of GNP
1956	20.0	21.5	0.093
1957	45.0	—	—
1958	45.0	32.7	0.138
1959	65.0	37.8	0.172
1960	67.78	47.8	0.142
1961	77.78	55.2	0.141
1962	76.39	60.2	0.127
1963	77.77	71.1	0.109
1964	72.37	82.4	0.088
1965	72.37	91.1	0.079
1966	89.57	106.7	0.084
1967	94.57	125.9	0.075
1968	94.57	148.2	0.064
1969	100.01	174.9	0.057
1970	87.39	203.4	0.043
1971	77.14	228.0	0.034
1972	71.70	310.3	0.023
1973	71.70	400.4	0.018
1974	71.70	n.a.	n.a.
1975	71.70	n.a.	n.a.
1976	41.70	n.a.	n.a.
1977	11.30	n.a.	n.a.

Note: n.a.= data not available

Source: Office of Japanese prime minister, Japan Statistical Yearbook: 1972, p. 487 (reparation figures represents commitments); Japan, Economic Planning Agency, Japanese Economic Indicators, no. 266 (April 1974), p. 40.

TABLE 4.4

Indices of Japanese Real Gross National Product Per Capita
(1955: 100)

	Year	Index
Prewar	1935	87. 0
	1936	88. 6
	1937	109. 1
	1938	118. 8
	1939	111. 9
	1940	103. 7
Postwar	1947	54. 5
	1950	68. 8
	1951	75. 9
	1952	82. 9
	1953	89. 5
	1954	91. 1
	1955	100. 0
	1956	106. 2
	1957	115. 2
	1958	114. 1
	1959	133. 7
	1960	150. 7

Source: Alan H. Gleason, "Economic Growth and Consumption in Japan, " in William W. Lockwood, ed. , The State and Economic Enterprise in Japan (Princeton: Princeton University Press, 1965), pp. 434-36.

countries, however, insisted that reparations include the provision of equipment. Japan finally agreed to provide goods to the extent that such provision would not cause severe adverse effects in her balance of payments. All of the reparations procurements, however, were tied to both Japanese goods and services. Furthermore the Japanese were more concerned with the possibility that the reparations might serve to replace the normal export flow from Japan.

This can be analyzed by noting, first, the extent of reparations actually paid in comparison with the total amount of Japanese exports, and, second, the share of reparations goods and services in the total imports of the recipient countries. The share of actual reparations in the total Japanese export figure has been about 1. 5 percent, as shown in Table 4. 5.

Reparations amounted to as much as 2. 5 percent of Japanese exports in 1960 and declined after that as the total amount of regular

49

TABLE 4. 5

Japanese Reparations Payments, Exports, and Reparations
As a Percentage of Exports

Year	Reparations ($million)	Japanese Exports ($billion)	Reparations as Percent of Exports
1956	3. 9	2, 598	0. 15
1957	49. 8	2, 913	1. 7
1958	47. 4	2, 895	1. 6

Source: Baisho Mondai, Kenkyukai, Nippon no Baisho: Sono
Genjo to Mondai-ten (Tokyo: Gaiko Jihosha, 1959), p. 220.

Japanese exports expanded. Thus in terms of total exports the reparations payments eventually counted little. In addition, to minimize any
adverse effects on regular exports, the Japanese encouraged purchases
of capital goods and services that would not have normally been
ordered by the recipient countries in regular trade. The reparations
agreement for Indonesia, for example, specifically provided that the
reparations had to be implemented so as not to hinder the regular
trade between Japan and Indonesia or upset the balance-of-payments
position of Japan. [13] As a result of this policy the major portion of the
baisho payments for Indonesia was directed, as shown in Table 4. 6,
to the procurement of goods and services needed for construction of
factories, department stores, bridges, buildings, and shipyards.
In addition to the goods and services provided as reparation items
Indonesia received the equivalent of $81. 7 million worth of goods
and services from funds made available as a corollary to the reparation
funds.

Similarly the bulk of items provided to Burma in both reparations
and reparation-like payments consisted of such capital goods as
vehicles (trains), machinery, and other equipment that Burma could
not have purchased otherwise (see Table 4. 7). Burma utilized 10, 390
million yen, or about $30 million, for the construction of an electric
power station at Balu-Chaung. More than 230 Japanese technicians
were employed in the designing and construction of the dam. Some
of the major Burmese projects, aimed at setting up plants and factories
for truck assembly, electric equipment, and agricultural machinery,
were furthered by the reparation-like payments.

Thus the implementation of the reparations agreements made
possible a massive flow of Japanese industrial products to the recipient
countries in Southeast Asia. By the early 1960s Southeast Asia offered
Japan her greatest export potentials, as Japan had lost her major markets in China and Korea following World War II. The baisho acted as
an inducement for Japanese exports to Southeast Asia: while Japan

50

TABLE 4. 6

Japanese Reparations to Indonesia, by Purposes
(billion yen)

Purpose	Amount
River and areas development	109. 1
Steel sheet factory	64. 6
Plywood factory	23. 9
Textile factory	32. 7
Hotel construction	74. 8
Department store construction	37. 2
Building construction	20. 8
Bridge construction	33. 8
Shipyards	22. 6
Machinery	267. 1
Consumer goods	33. 6
Educational training programs	30. 6
Negotiations and delegates expenses, etc.	52. 0
Total	802. 0
	($223 million)

Source: Tsusansho, Keizai Kyoryoku no Genjo to Mondaidi 1971,
p. 307.

TABLE 4. 7

Japanese Reparations and Reparation-like Payments
to Burma, by Purposes
(million yen)

Purpose	Amount
Balu-Chaung electric power station	10, 390
Large and medium truck assembly and passenger car plants	2, 530
Small truck assembly plants	3, 295
Home electric appliance assembly factories	3, 095
Agricultural machinery factories	1, 589
Electric machinery and equipment	5, 857
Vehicles (trains)	8, 353
Textile machinery	2, 547

Source: Gaimusho, Biruma no Jiryoku Kosei Rosen to Wagakuni
no Keizei Kyoryoku (Tokyo, 1972), pp. 143-44.

51

had to provide industrial products free of charge under the reparations agreements, the introduction of these products in a number of Asian countries was to bring about demands for follow-up orders as local markets geared to the Japanese products were formed and expanded. As a result of this stimulus provided by the baisho, Japanese exports to Southeast Asian countries increased substantially starting in the late 1950s: Exports to the Philippines more than doubled between 1955 and 1962. What is especially notable in Japanese trade patterns since around 1957 is the decline in the export of Japanese textiles and other light manufacturing goods to Southeast Asia and the corresponding rise in the export of metal products, machinery, and chemicals. Shipments of cement plants, ships, rolling stock, and other heavy goods were made possible by the reparations payments. In the case of Indonesia reparations also formed a large share of the increase in Japanese exports. Reparations payments thus opened the way to wider trade in capital as well as consumer goods.

NOTES

1. Edwin O. Reischauer, The United States and Japan (New York: Viking Press, 1965), p. 288.

2. Reischauer, op. cit., pp. 370-71.

3. Yoshiyuki Hagiwara, "Towareru Nihon no tai-Ajia Shisei-ekonomikku man' e no tenkan ga hitsuyo," Economisto, March 17, 1970, pp. 14-21, trans. Andrew Horvat, "Economic Animal Reconsidered", The Japan Interpreter, Spring 1972, p. 142.

4. Baisho Mondai Kenkyukai, ed., Nippon no Baisho: Sono Genjo to Mondai-ten (Tokyo: Gaiko Jihosha, 1959), pp. 11-18. Japan also agreed to pay reparations to Switzerland, Spain, Sweden, and Denmark for "damages" inflicted upon their property during the war; payments amounted to one to six million dollars each.

5. Ibid. in "Hashigaki (Preface)".

6. Kakuten Hara, Kankoku Keizai no Kiseki (Tokyo: Nippon Kokusai Mondai Kenkyujo, 1970), pp. 71-72.

7. Gaimusho, Waga gaiko no kinkyo: Showa 48-nen do (Tokyo: 1973), pp. 506-07.

8. Aikhiro Kasai, "Chugoku wa neze Baisho o toranakattaka," Chuo Koron March 1974, pp. 93-101.

9. Lawrence Olson, Japan in Postwar Asia (New York: Praeger, 1970), p. 29.

10. Reischauer, op. cit., p. 370.

11. Olson, op. cit., pp. 15-26.

12. Baisho Mondai Kenkyukai, op. cit., p. 28.

13. Baisho Mondai Kenkyukai, op. cit., p. 220.

DISTRIBUTION
AND VALUATION
OF AID RESOURCES

To attain her varying aid objectives Japan has provided aid resources to a number of less-developed countries, as noted previously. Both the extent and content of the aid provided have changed over years and differed widely from one country to another. While some recipient countries have received a considerable amount of Japanese technical assistance, others have received mostly capital aid in the form of development loans and export credits. The kinds and terms of aid provided to respective recipient countries show the extent of importance attached by Japan to each recipient's aid.

The Japanese preference for any particular recipient country may be ascertained in terms of the overall value of aid resources she provides to that country. First, the value of such aid is determined by its differing kinds and magnitudes (technical assistance differs in its importance from capital aid). Second, while the extent of capital aid is shown in aid statistics as financial resources, their nominal values differ significantly from real values because of varying terms. To assess the real value of capital aid a valuation methodology, as noted in Chapter 3, is a useful instrument for determining the extent of "sacrifice" incurred by the donor (Japan) in each aid provision; it permits a quantitative measurement of the nature of aid decisions made by the donor.

This chapter will present, first, the principles of the valuation methodology and, then, the actual measurement of each loan extended by official Japanese development assistance agencies—the Export-Import Bank of Japan and the Overseas Economic Cooperation Fund (OECF)—to point out which countries have been given preferential aid treatment by Japan.

THE VALUATION METHODOLOGY

The value of an aid loan is assessed by measuring its grant element and value. The grant value of a loan is the difference between the face value of the loan and the present value of amortization and interest payments, discounted at an appropriate rate of interest reflecting the opportunity cost of capital in either the donor or recipient country. The grant element is the grant value expressed as a share of the face value of the loan. The grant element and value of the aid loan represent the extent of present cost to the donor if the donor's opportunity cost of capital is used as a rate of discount.

The most concise approach in finding the grant element and value was formulated by Goran Ohlin. [1] According to Ohlin, the grant element, GE, and the grant value, GV, are found by solving the following equations that accommodate the possibility of a loan's grace period:

$$GE = (1 - \frac{i}{q}) \left(1 - \frac{e^{-q^G} - e^{-q^T}}{q(T - G)} \right)$$

$$GV = L(1 - \frac{i}{q}) \left(1 - \frac{e^{-q^G} - e^{-q^T}}{q(T - G)} \right)$$

where L = face value of loan
i = interest rate
q = discount rate
G = grace period
T = maturity time
e = 2.719 (base of natural logarithm)

Figure 1 shows, as an example of this, the grant value of a loan with its face value, $30 million. Abbreviations are given to indicate the following payments:

NTAP = nominal total aggregate payment
NAPR = nominal aggregate principal repayment
PVTAP = present value of total aggregate payment
NAIP = nominal aggregate interest payment
NAPR = nominal annual principal repayment
NAIP = nominal annual interest payment

With the interest rate of 3 percent per year and the grace period of 5 years, the aggregate interest payments would nominally amount to $4.5 million at the end of the grace period as indicated by line NAIP.

FIGURE 1

Aid Loan Values and Payments

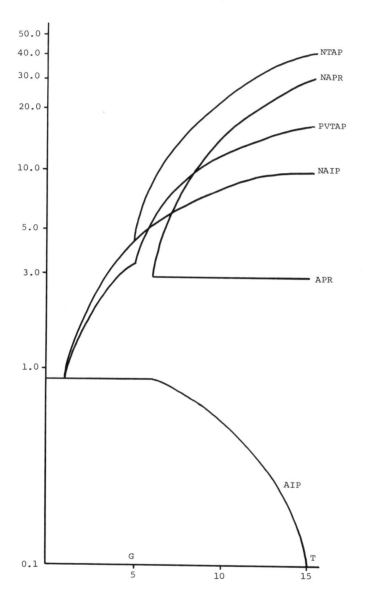

The total aggregate amount of payments of principal and interest payments are completed at the end of the maturity period of 15 years (see line NTAP). If the value of each payment is discounted at the annual rate of 10 percent, the present value of total aggregate payments would be only $17.10 million as shown by line PVTAP.

The difference between the face value of the loan and the present value of total aggregate payments, which would now amount to about $13 million, is the grant value of the aid loan. The grant element representing the grant value as a share of the face value of the loan would be 0.4316, or 43.16 percent. In the present case the loan cost and benefit are equal in quantity since the uniform discount rate is used. The magnitudes of the cost and benefit are calculated by simply using the different rates of discount prevailing in the countries concerned. To distinguish two kinds of grant values and elements, those which indicate the cost to the donor are termed grant cost-value (GCV) and grant cost-element (GCE). The GCV and GCE are then measured to ascertain the extent of burden the donor shoulders in providing aid loans.

Grant Cost-Element and Grant Cost-Value as Indicators of
Foreign Aid Policy

Intertemporal and interrecipient-country comparisons of grant cost-elements and grant cost-values help identify any consistency or changes taking place in the aid policy of a donor country. The relationship between GCE-GCV and the aid policy is ascertained in terms of two propositions.

The first of these propositions is that given the equal size of aid loans, the larger the GCE of either one of them, the greater the burden shouldered by a donor in extending the loan with the larger GCE. The extent of favorable aid treatment given by a donor is measured by determining changes in the magnitudes of GCE over time. If a donor provides two aid loans of the same magnitude to two countries or regions, and the GCE of one loan is larger than that of the other, the country or region receiving the former loan is designated as receiving preferential, or more favorable, treatment.

The second proposition is that the aggregate amount of favorable treatment shown by a donor is larger for recipient country A than B if A receives a greater amount GCV than B does. This proposition is designed to accommodate the possibility that recipient countries receive different amounts of aid loans at varying terms. In reality most aid loans are extended in this way under different conditions. The relative magnitudes of favorable treatment extended by the donor may then be measured by comparing GCV's for respective recipient countries.

56

Computation of Japanese Aid Loans

This section will outline the procedure adopted for calculating the GCE and GCV of Japanese aid loans, analyze the outcome of the calculation in terms of the propositions noted above, and compare the GCE's and GCV's for respective recipient countries and regions to ascertain the trend in Japanese aid policy. Throughout the section comparative data would be examined to test the basic hypothesis that Japan extends preferential treatment to such countries as those with rich energy and natural resources. We also attempt to identify reasons for undertaking such a policy.

Choice of Loans and Discount Rates

Japan has provided both official and private loans and credits. She has also made a number of reparation and reparation-like payments arising out of World War II. While they amounted to more than $15 billion in total, such an item as the baisho represented a price of war settlement as ascertained in Chapter IV did not represent a voluntary action of Japan to assist the economic and social development of recipient countries. The private loans and credits are extended mainly for the purpose of expanding Japanese investment and increasing export from Japan. As pointed out in Chapter III, clear indicators of the donor government's intention and willingness are official development assistance loans designed to promote the economic and social development of recipient countries. We have, therefore, included for the purpose of computation those development assistance loans provided by the Japanese government through mostly Export-Import Bank of Japan, Overseas Economic Co-operation Fund and some city banks. Selection of the loans has been made based on the information given in a government white paper on economic cooperation produced by Tsusansho. [2]

The decision to compute only ODA loans in this study is in contrast to other studies made on the valuation of Japanese aid. John Pincus, for example, simply accepted an estimate based on "typical terms and conditions" because he lacked specific data when he computed, among other items, the "real" value of Japanese aid from the years 1961 and 1962. [3] Ohlin similarly computed the real cost of overall aid commitments made by Japan in 1963 and compared it with those of other countries: no information is provided on the individual recipients of Japanese aid. [4] OECD figured the grant elements of ODA loans based on the discount rate of 10 percent as an approximate rate of economic return. [5] And Martha Loutfi calculated the "present" value of Japanese aid, including loans and grants for the years from 1958 to 1968. In selecting a discount rate she decided to adopt the interest rate on Japanese Telephone and Telegraph Company bonds, and since the interest rate fluctuated between 7.70 percent and 14.01 percent, she chose to estimate the present value of Japanese aid at the two discount rates of 8 percent and 15 percent. [6]

In this study the grant element and value of each loan has been computed for the period from 1958, when the first Japanese loan was extended to India, to November 1973. Instead of adopting varying discount rates prevailing at different points in time, this study employed the discount rate of 10 percent, following the example of DAC. The choice of this particular discount rate may not always serve to determine the precise amount of GCE and GCV for each loan under changing economic conditions. But the uniform application of a single discount rate serves the purpose of this study, which is to ascertain how much preferential treatment is accorded by Japan in her extending of aid resources to certain countries.

Analysis of Computation Results

During the period from 1958 to November 1973, Japan granted a total of 158 development assistance loans amounting to $4,713.5 million in face value (see appendix B). The computation of these loans resulted in several notable findings, some of them confirming certain aid claims of the Japanese government and others revealing changes in both the direction and nature of Japanese aid that are not yet commonly recognized.

First, this computation confirmed the claim of the Japanese government that both the face and grant value of Japanese aid loans increased substantially during the 1958-73 period. However, in this growth pattern upward turns took place in 1965 and 1971 for reasons which the Japanese government has not been vocal about, thus showing the political nature of the Japanese aid program and how the program is used extensively by the Japanese government for the attainment of current national objectives. Second, this study found that the major part of Japanese aid loans continues to be channeled to Asian countries, although several countries in other continents began to receive an increasing number and amount of loans in the early 1970s. Moreover within Asia, the aid preference accorded to the Far East and South Asia in the early 1960s has been shifted to Southeast Asia. Third, as noted in Chapter 3, there has been a general easing of the terms of loans, reflecting various efforts in this direction made by the Japanese government to respond affirmatively to international pressures exerted by the United Nations Conference on Trade and Development (UNCTAD), DAC and the Pearson Commission. Fourth, while Japan seems to have established no detailed criteria for determining the exact amount and terms of loans for developing countries with different levels of development, she has provided softer loans to such relatively less developed countries as Indonesia and Burma and harder loans to such relatively more developed countries as Brazil and Mexico. The total face value of Japanese loans extended annually, though fluctuating noticeably from year to year, grew substantially over the entire 1958-73 period. During the last few years of the period the amount of lending increased rapidly and as a result the aggregate cumulative amount of loans at face value increased from $1.7 billion in August 1969 to $2.5 billion in September 1971 and to $4.7 billion in November 1973. [7]

New impetus in the growth of Japanese aid loans appeared especially in 1965 and 1971; in both these years the value of loans extended more than tripled. It increased from $123 million in 1964 to $448 million in 1965 and from $181 million in 1970 to $697 million in 1971. As shown in Table 5.1, the enormous increase in Japanese loans in these years can be more clearly seen in the large amount of grant cost-value recorded for the loans, or in the large amount of "sacrifice"

TABLE 5.1

Face Value and Grant Cost-Value of
Japanese Loans, 1958-73 (million dollars)

Fiscal Year	Face Value	Grant Cost-Value
1958	50.0	8.76
1959	3.8	0.69
1960	7.5	0.75
1961	117.5	28.32
1962	25.0	6.17
1963	110.0	28.59
1964	122.6	29.52
1965	448.4	159.79
1966	272.3	72.70
1967	242.0	75.63
1968	238.2	92.85
1969	189.3	70.55
1970	181.0	69.76
1971	1,008.5	406.77
1972	1,137.8	467.67
1973	559.6	238.87
Total	4,713.5	1,757.39

Note: The figures for 1973 represent amounts for eight months from April 1, 1973 to November 30, 1973. The Japanese fiscal year starts on April 1 and ends on March 31 of the following year.
Source: Compiled by author from Appendix B.

59

incurred by the Japanese lenders. The grant cost-value of $159.8 million in 1965 was more than five times that of $29.5 million recorded in 1964, and the amount of grant cost-value in 1971 was nearly six times that of 1970.

These distinctive upward turns in 1965 and 1971 were deliberately spurred by the Japanese government in its desire to both protect Japan's kokueki (national interest) and attain her existing national goals. These goals were, in the middle of the 1960s, the establishment of a leadership role in the Asian region and in the early 1970s, the sustaining of Japan's domestic prosperity and societal welfare by securing essential supplies of raw materials and energy resources and preventing any further environmental deterioration.

The sharp increase in 1965 resulted from the extension of large loans to South Korea and Taiwan. In the case of South Korea, Japan agreed to provide a $200 million loan to assist in the improvement of railroads, shipping, highways, and a steel mill in Korea. The real significance of the loan agreement, however, lies in the fact that it was negotiated as part of the process to establish diplomatic relations between the two countries. Similarly Japan agreed to extend a loan amounting to $150 million to Taiwan for the explicit purpose of assisting in the implementation of a fourth four-year development plan in Taiwan; the loan funds were to be used specifically for the improvement of the Tsengwen dam, the Kaohsiung harbor, and Taiwan's communication facilities and power distribution networks. But in reality the loan signified Japan's undertaking of katagawari (see Chapter 1) as the United States had decided to terminate her economic aid to Taiwan in 1965. [8] It is notable that 1965 was also a watershed in terms of Japanese-Indonesian relations with the ousting of Sukarno as Indonesia's president. As Sukarno's successor, Suharto consolidated his control of Indonesia and reversed the Country's previous anti-Western policy. Japan then took the initiative in reviving a consortium to finance loans to Indonesia. In addition to the subsequent improvement of politico-diplomatic relations between the two countries, Indonesia's rich natural resources induced Japan to extend aid to Indonesia and thereby secure her resources for Japan's own growing raw material and energy resource needs.

Japan's ever-increasing needs for supplies from abroad in fact constituted one of the two reasons why the Japanese government decided to further expand both the total amount and geographic coverage of aid loans. Thus while the total face value of Japanese loans was a few hundred million dollars a year in the 1960s, it became more than $1 billion a year starting in 1971. And the total cumulative number of countries receiving Japanese aid loans was 24 in 1969, but increased to 36 by 1973. In 1969 countries that had received cumulative Japanese loans numbered 14 in Asia (Afghanistan, Burma, the Khmer Republic (Cambodia), India, Indonesia, Iran, Phillipines, Pakistan, South Korea, South Vietnam, Sri Lanka, Taiwan, Malaysia, and Thailand);

5 in Latin America (Argentina, Brazil, Chile, Mexico, and Paraguay); 4 in Africa (Kenya, Nigeria, Tanzania, and Uganda); and 1 in Europe (Yugoslavia). By 1973, 12 countries had been added to this list: 2 (Singapore and Nepal) in Asia; 3 (Colombia, Costa Rica, and Peru) in Latin America; 4 (Ethiopia, Madagascar, Zaire, and Zambia) in Africa; 1 (Turkey) in Europe; and 2 (Syria and Egypt) in the Middle East.

Another cause of the sharp increase in Japanese aid loans was the Japanese desire to transfer some of its manufacturing activities to other nations in order to minimize the adverse effects of continuing heavy industrialization in Japan. This industrialization had spurred the expansion of Japanese exports and the accumulation of foreign exchange, but at the same time necessitated ever-increasing supplies of raw materials and energy resources and caused a deterioration in environmental conditions in Japan. By the end of the 1960s, which was known in Japan as the decade of the income-doubling plan, environmental deterioration became so damaging to the societal welfare of Japan that the Japanese government had to begin taking a number of steps aimed at reducing the negative effects of heavy industrialization: one of these steps was the transfer of certain manufacturing activities to other countries. The impact of such a step on the nature and direction of Japanese foreign aid has been far-reaching, as will be examined in Chapter 6.

As noted above, it was found in this study that the major portion of Japanese aid loans continually goes to Asian countries and that Southeast Asia has emerged as the largest recipient subregion within Asia. In 1969 Asia received $1,580 million, or 90 percent, of the total cumulative amount of Japanese loans in face value, while Latin America received $104 million, or 5.9 percent, Africa received $44 million, or 2.5 percent, and other areas $25 million, or 1.4 percent. As shown in Table 5.2, the cumulative face value amount of loans received by Asian countries increased to $3,720 million by November 1973, but the Asian share of total Japanese loans in face value declined to less than 80 percent as the amounts and percentages of loans to Latin America, Africa, and Europe increased substantially.

Within the Asian region the share of loans going to Southeast Asia continued to expand substantially, while the shares for other subregions declined noticeably. As shown in Table 5.3, the share for Southeast Asia measured against total Japanese loans for the world increased from 27.0 percent in August 1969 to 40.7 percent by November 1973, as a result of a fourfold increase in the face value of loans extended to Southeast Asia. The share for the Far Eastern region (South Korea and Taiwan) decreased from 20.0 percent in August 1969 to 12.5 percent in November 1973, although the face value of loans to the Far East increased from $350.0 million to $590 million. Similarly the share for South Asia decreased from 42.1

TABLE 5.2

Cumulative Face Value of Japanese Aid Loans
to Various Regions, 1969 and 1973 (million dollars)

Region	1969		1973	
	Face Value	Percent of Total	Face Value	Percent of Total
Asia	1,575.9	90.2	3,717.8	78.6
Latin America	103.6	5.9	538.3	11.5
Africa	44.0	2.5	242.6	5.2
Middle East	—*	—*	54.4	1.1
Europe	5.0	0.3	77.4	1.6
International organizations	20.0	1.1	83.0	1.8
Total	1,748.5	100.0	4,713.5	100.0

*: As of 1969 no Middle Eastern countries had received cumulative Japanese loans.
Source: Tsusansho, Keizai Kyoryoku no Genjo to Mondai -ten 1969, p. 122, and 1973, p. 168.

TABLE 5.3

Cumulative Face Value of Japanese Aid Loans to
Asian Subregions and Other Regions, 1969 and 1973 (million dollars)

Region	1969		1973	
	Face Value	Percent of Total	Face Value	Percent of Total
Asia	1,575.9	90.2	3,717.8	78.9
Far East	350.0	20.0	589.7	12.5
Southeast Asia	470.3	27.0	1,925.1	40.7
South Asia	736.6	42.1	1,184.0	25.1
Southwest Asia	19.0	1.1	19.0	0.4
Other regions	172.6	9.8	995.7	21.3
Total	1,748.5	100.0	4,713.5	100.0

Source: Compiled by the author from Table 5.2.

TABLE 5.4

Cumulative Face Value of Japanese Aid Loans
Received by Various Countries, by Rank Order: November 1973
(million dollars)

Country	Amount	Country	Amount
Indonesia	1,055.0	Yugoslavia	35.0
India	802.9	Zambia	30.0
South Korea	413.5	Syria	28.8
Pakistan	323.5	Egypt	25.6
Brazil	322.5	Chile	17.9
Thailand	267.8	Iran	17.0
Philippines	180.4	Kenya	16.6
Taiwan	176.2	Paraguay	16.5
Burma	169.9	Costa Rica	14.0
Malaysia	167.0	Madagascar	13.6
Zaire	112.0	ECIE	13.4
Mexico	80.1	Ethiopia	12.0
Peru	74.5	Argentina	10.2
IDB	69.6	Tanzania	5.6
Sri Lanka (Ceylon)	56.3	Khmer Republic (Cambodia)	4.2
Nigeria	50.0	Uganda	2.6
Turkey	42.4	Colombia	2.6
South Vietnam	40.8	Afghanistan	2.0
Singapore	40.0	Nepal	1.0

Source: Tsusansho, Keizai Kyoryoku no Genjo to Mondai-ten
1973, p. 168.

percent in August 1969 to 25.1 percent in November 1973 in spite of
an increase of $47 million in the face value of loans received by this
subregion.

Among individual countries, Indonesia, Brazil, Burma, and the
Philippines saw the amount of their loans from Japan increase more
noticeably than any other recipient countries; the face value of the
total cumulative amount of loans received by these four countries
combined as of November 1973 had reached more than five times the
amount they had received by August 1969. Among the four, Indonesia
presented by far the most remarkable case. While she had received
no loans before 1966, Indonesia became the largest recipient of
Japanese aid loans by 1973, as shown in Table 5.4.

The third distinctive feature of the growth pattern of Japanese
aid loans, as noted previously, is a general easing of the terms of
the loans. As pointed out in the discussion of valuation methodology
earlier in this chapter, the more concessional the terms of loans are,

64

the higher would be the grant cost-element of loans. Table 5. 5 shows the weighted grant cost-element of Japanese loans for each fiscal year from 1958 to 1973. In spite of fluctuations in the face value of loans extended from year to year, the grant cost-element rose steadily from 17. 5 percent in 1958 to 42. 7 percent in 1973, reflecting a softening of loan terms. However, the grant cost-element of 42 percent attained by Japan in 1972 was about 15 percent below the average rate of 57 percent for DAC members as a whole; and only four countries, Austria (38 percent), France (32 percent), Italy (20 percent), and Portugal (32 percent), extended ODA loans with terms harder than those of Japan. Major donors that extended loans in 1972 with a grant cost-element of 20-to-30 percent higher than that of Japan included Canada (90 percent), Sweden (80 percent), the United States (65 percent), the United Kingdom (64 percent), and Germany (60 percent). [9]

A general, but rather slow, improvement in the terms of Japanese loans reflected Japan's attitude of otsukiai (see Chapter 1); under the aforementioned international pressure the Japanese government reluctantly followed the course of a general easing of loan terms but only to the minimal extent expected of Japan as a member of kokusai shakai (the international community).

The fourth characteristic of Japanese aid loans—the varying degrees of "sacrifice" incurred by Japan in extending development loans—was ascertained in this study by computing the amount of grant cost-element and grant cost-value of each of the 158 loans extended by Japan from 1958 to 1973. This computation reveals that Japan incurred the largest amount of "sacrifice" in extending development loans to Southeast Asian countries, and that Japan's preference for particular recipients, which changed over the 15-year period, is being increasingly directed to countries that are relatively less developed but endowed with rich natural resources.

TABLE 5. 5

Grant Cost-Element of Japanese Aid Loans, 1958-73 (percentage)

Year	Grant Cost-Element	Year	Grant Cost-Element
1958	17. 52	1966	26. 70
1959	18. 08	1967	31. 25
1960	19. 85	1968	38. 98
1961	24. 10	1969	37. 26
1962	24. 66	1970	38. 53
1963	25. 99	1971	40. 33
1964	24. 08	1972	41. 96
1965	35. 64	1973	42. 65

Source: Compiled by the author from Appendix B.

65

As shown in Table 5. 6, Southeast Asian countries were provided with loans containing such a relatively high grant cost-element that three of these countries, Thailand, Burma, and Malaysia, obtained more in grant cost-value than a few other countries that received loans which were larger in face value. Thailand received loans totaling $167. 8 million in face value, Burma obtained loans of $169. 9 million in face value, and Malaysia got $167. 0 million; they ranked, respectively, sixth, ninth, and tenth in the list of the largest recipients in terms of the face value of Japanese loans. In terms of the grant cost-value of the loans, however, the three countries were, respectively, fourth, six, and eighth. Indonesia's grant cost-element was 10 percent more than India's, but Indonesia's grant cost-value of loans was nearly twice that of India while the face value of her loans was only about 25 percent larger than that of India. In the cases of Pakistan and Burma, their grant cost-value was about the same, in spite of the fact that the face value of loans received by Burma was a little more than half of that received by Pakistan. Both Brazil and Mexico received a substantial amount of loans in face value, but the actual amount of "sacrifice" incurred by Japan on these loans was small as their terms were kept close to those currently prevailing in the commercial market. Brazil received $322. 5 million in loans but the grant cost-value of these loans turned out to be only $55. 5 million as their weighted grant cost-element was kept at only 17. 22 percent. Similarly the grant cost-value of loans received by Mexico reached only $13. 2 million, due to a low grant cost-element of 16. 46 percent, in spite of the fact that the face value of these loans hit $80. 1 million.

Those countries accorded the most preferential treatment (a weighted grant cost-element of 40 percent or more) by Japan were Asian and African countries, with the exception of Syria. About half of these were Southeast Asian countries —Burma, Indonesia, Thailand, the Philippines, South Vietnam, and the Khmer Republic. Also included in the group of most-favored recipients were one country from the Far East (South Korea), one from West Asia (Afghanistan), and three African countries (Ethiopia, Madagascar, and Zaire). All of these countries are relatively less developed countries that showed per capita income of less than $300 a year in 1971.

The tendency of Japan to give greater preference to countries that are relatively less developed, but that are endowed with vital natural resources needed by Japan, has emerged since the middle of the 1960s. This trend was clearly observed when we examined changes over time in the grant cost-element of Japanese aid loans. The major countries that received loans with a cumulative face value of more than $50 million during the period from 1958 to 1973 may be divided into four groups according to changes of the grant cost-element of the loans.

TABLE 5.6

Grant Cost-Element and Grant Cost-Value of
Japanese Aid Loans, by Recipient Countries

Country, by Nominal Ranking	Grant Cost-Element (percent)	Grant Cost-Value ($ million)	Actual Ranking
1. Indonesia	42.11	444.30	1
2. India	30.39	243.99	2
3. South Korea	40.40	167.05	3
4. Pakistan	27.14	88.77	5
5. Brazil	17.22	55.52	9
6. Thailand	41.73	161.76	4
7. Philippines	40.02	81.22	7
8. Taiwan	27.91	49.18	11
9. Burma	52.38	88.75	6
10. Malaysia	38.02	63.49	8
11. Zaire	46.18	51.72	10
12. Mexico	16.46	13.18	18
13. Peru	35.36	26.35	12
14. IDB	19.00	13.22	17
15. Sri Lanka	32.20	18.13	13
16. Nigeria	32.01	16.00	15
17. Turkey	36.02	14.91	16
18. South Vietnam	43.75	17.85	14
19. Singapore	30.24	12.10	20
20. Yugoslavia	24.21	8.47	22
21. Zambia	37.91	11.37	21
22. Syria	42.33	12.20	19
23. Egypt	23.21	5.94	23
24. Chile	21.25	3.80	30
25. Iran	26.19	4.45	29
26. Kenya	34.47	5.72	26
27. Paraguay	35.84	5.91	24
28. Costa Rica	37.91	5.31	27
29. Madagascar	43.32	5.90	25
30. BCIE	15.54	1.09	34
31. Ethiopia	43.32	5.20	28
32. Argentina	15.11	1.54	33
33. Tanzania	28.07	1.57	34
34. Khmer Republic	44.58	1.87	31
35. Uganda	28.07	0.79	36
36. Colombia	14.08	0.37	37
37. Afghanistan	41.15	0.823	35
38. Nepal	24.12	0.24	38

Note: The nominal ranking is determined according to the total
cumulative amount of loans received. The actual ranking is found
according to the grant cost-value of loans.

Source: Compiled by the author from Appendix B.

67

The first group are the Southeast Asian countries of India, Pakistan, and Sri Lanka (Ceylon). These countries have been receiving Japanese development loans from their early stages —India since 1958, Pakistan since 1961, and Sri Lanka since 1966. Japan extended aid loans to these countries for three main reasons. First, during the early stages of Japanese aid India and Pakistan constituted valuable markets for Japanese capital goods until the Far Eastern and Southeast Asian countries began to replace them as promising markets. Second, as admitted by the Japanese Ministry of International Trade and Industry (Tsusansho), the Japanese government was conscious of the fact that as a member of the aid consortia for India and Pakistan, Japan was expected to contribute adequately as part of <u>otsukiai</u> and therby fulfill her share of aid responsibility. [10] Most of the loans to these countries, therefore, were extended in consultation with the consortia and were meant for commodity purchases rather than project executions. A few projects financed by Japanese loans were directed for the improvement of infrastructure facilities and the exploitation of mineral resources and petroleum. Third, India and Pakistan provided Japan with certain mineral and agricultural products. For example India's exports of iron ore to Japan amounted to $199 million in 1970 and $219 million in 1972. In addition India exported manganese to Japan valued at $14 million in 1972, and the export of cotton from India and Pakistan amounted to more than $21 million and $59 million, respectively, in 1972. Both India and Pakistan also exported a substantial amount of frozen shrimp for consumption in Japan ($40 million from India and $9 million from Pakistan). While their overall trade with Japan was substantial for India and Pakistan, their importance to Japan declined over the years in comparison with Southeast Asian countries. [11]

The Japanese government was fully aware of this trend and re-directed its aid emphasis to Southeast Asian countries. This policy change is reflected in changes in the grant cost-value and grant cost-element of Japanese loans to India and Pakistan. As noted above, the share of the grant cost-value of loans to these countries in the entire Japanese aid loan program declined over the 15-year period (1958-73). The grant cost-element for India, Pakistan, and Sri Lanka improved over the period, but the rate of rise was not as high as that of loans for Southeast Asian countries. As shown in Table 5.7, the first loan to India made in 1958 had a grant cost-element of 17.5 percent. After that the grant cost-element rose to 24.7 percent in 1961, to 26.2 percent in 1963, and to 30.7 percent by 1968. It climbed further to 37.9 percent in 1971 and to more than 40 percent for loans extended in 1973. Similarly the first two loans to Pakistan in 1961 and 1962 carried a grant cost-element of 24.7 percent each. The next four loans (extended up to 1967), with a face value of $30 million each, had a grant cost-element of 26.2 percent. The grant cost-element subsequently rose to 31.4 percent for Pakistan by the late 1960s, and climbed to 42.3 percent in 1972.

TABLE 5.7

Face Value and Grant Cost-Element of Japanese Aid Loans
to 3 Southeast Asian Countries

India

Year	Loan ($ million)	Grant Cost-Element (percent)
1958	50.0	17.52
1961	80.0	24.66
1963	15.0	24.66
1963	65.0	26.20
1964	60.0	26.20
1965	60.0	26.20
1966	42.5	26.20
1966	2.5	20.90
1967	7.0	26.20
1967	6.1	27.74
1967	38.9	29.73
1968	16.83	30.69
1968	28.17	31.37
1969	19.56	30.69
1969	25.44	31.37
1969	7.0	29.73
1970	25.4	30.69
1971	29.7	36.10
1971	18.0	32.57
1971	24.1	30.69
1971	100.6	37.91
1973	38.2	48.56
1973	42.9	42.33
Total	802.9	30.39

Pakistan

Year	Loan ($ million)	Grant Cost-Element (percent)
1961	20.0	24.66
1962	25.0	24.66
1963	30.0	26.20
1964	30.0	26.20
1966	30.0	26.20
1967	30.0	26.20
1967	30.0	29.72
1968	30.0	31.37
1969	30.0	31.37
1972	37.7	14.63
1972	4.3	37.91
1972	26.8	42.33
Total	323.8	27.14

Sri Lanka

Year	Loan ($ million)	Grant Cost-Element (percent)
1966	5.0	16.00
1966	5.0	16.00
1967	5.0	23.55
1968	5.0	31.37
1969	5.0	31.37
1971	5.0	36.10
1971	3.5	36.10
1972	11.4	37.91
1973	11.4	42.33
Total	56.3	32.20

Source: Compiled by author from Appendix B.

This level, however, was about 10 percent below the grant cost-element of loans extended by Japan to a second group of countries, which consisted mostly of Southeast Asian nations and a few African countries that were relatively less developed despite being endowed with vital mineral and energy resources and being exporters of substantial amounts of agricultural and fishery products (see Table 5. 8). Japan extended to these countries aid loans with a relatively large grant cost-element; major recipients in Asia were Indonesia, the Philippines, Thailand, and Burma, and, in Africa, Zaire and Nigeria. Japan extended such loans to these countries both to secure present and future supplies of certain mineral, agricultural, and fishery products and to minimize unbalanced trade, in favor of Japan, with two of the countries, Thailand and Burma.

Among this group of countries Indonesia has emerged as the largest Japanese loan recipient. This can be traced to the fact that Indonesia became the third largest exporter of oil to Japan by the end of the 1960s, topped only by Iran and Saudi Arabia. The value of Indonesian exports of oil to Japan amounted to $318 million in 1970; two years later it reached $648 million. As both the price and quantity of Indonesian oil exports to Japan increased substantially in both 1973 and 1974, their value was expected to double by 1974. The Japanese government was eager to secure as much oil from Indonesia as possible; thus a number of aid loan agreements were negotiated between Japan and Indonesia, including an agreement made by Prime Minister Sato and President Suharto in 1972 providing for the eventual extension by Japan of more than $200 million in development loans in exchange for 58 million kiloliters of oil from Indonesia. In addition to oil, Indonesia in 1972 supplied timber to Japan valued at $265 million, shrimp valued at $46 million, nickel at $16 million, and tin at $14 million. [12]

The Philippines has also been a major supplier of mineral and agricultural products to Japan. The export of copper and iron ore from the Philippines to Japan amounted to $169 million and $33 million, respectively, in 1970 and to $167 million and $158 million in 1958. Moreover Philippine timber and banana exports to Japan amounted to $167 million and $41 million, respectively, in 1972. Thailand meanwhile has exported mostly such agricultural and fishery prodicts as corn, shrimp, natural rubber, and jute; together exports of these products to Japan amounted to $25 million in 1972. As noted above, in the case of Thailand, the Japanese government was conscious of a heavy imbalance of trade in favor of Japan—Japanese exports had been twice the amount of imports from Thailand. Thus the Japanese government sought to use aid as a means of minimizing the adverse effects of this imbalance. Meanwhile this entire group of Southeast Asian countries became the major market for Japanese industrial products: Japan's exports of (largely) machinery, chemical, and metal products to Indonesia in 1973 amounted to $615 million; to

TABLE 5.8

Face Value and Grant Cost-Element of Japanese Aid Loans
to 6 Asian and African Countries

Year	Loan ($ million)	Grant Cost-Element (percent)	Year	Loan ($ million)	Grant Cost-Element (percent)
Indonesia			**Philippines**		
1966	30.0	21.26	1969	30.0	32.83
1967	50.0	36.10	1971	76.0	46.93
1967	45.0	29.40	1972	40.0	44.58
1968	75.0	50.54	1973	34.4	51.95
1968	7.0	29.40	Total	180.4	45.02
1969	75.0	50.54	**Burma**		
1969	6.6	29.40	1969	30.0	44.58
1970	100.0	50.54	1971	11.8	53.88
1971	151.9	53.88	1972	15.0	53.88
1971	109.5	44.64	1972	65.4	53.88
1972	175.5	53.88	1973	10.0	53.88
1973	74.7	53.88	1973	37.7	53.88
1973	9.7	53.88	Total	169.9	52.38
1973	145.1	60.96	**Nigeria**		
Total	1,055.0	42.11	1966	30.0	28.07
Thailand			1972	20.0	37.91
1968	30.0	37.72	Total	50.0	32.01
1968	30.0	26.20	**Zaire**		
1972	110.4	48.74	1973	112.0	46.18
1972	26.0	48.74			
1972	39.0	36.56			
1972	32.4	36.56			
Total	267.8	41.73			

Source: Compiled by the author from Appendix B.

the Philippines $457 million; and to Thailand $522 million. However, while Indonesia and the Philippines enjoyed some trade surpluses with Japan, Thailand suffered a continuous trade deficit vis-a-vis Japan.

Burma presents a rather exceptional case among these Southeast Asian countries. As she had adopted the socialist system of government, Burma's trade with Japan remained relatively small during the postwar era. Japanese investments in Burma were also virtually non-existent over most of these years. However, when Japan made reparation payments to Burma and provided accompanying economic cooperation funds, she became the largest donor of aid to Burma. Burma at the same time remained friendly to Japan even after World War II. More crucial, Burma was known to possess substantial mineral and petroleum resources. Conscious of this, the Japanese government extended a number of aid loans to Burma aimed at exploring Burmese offshore oil deposits and at the establishment of automobile assembly and agricultural machinery assembly plants in Burma; these loans were granted at concessional terms. [13]

Japan has also begun to rely on Africa for supplies of oil and mineral resources. As the Japanese demand for oil increased rapidly, so did its imports from oil-producing countries in Africa. For example as oil production in Nigeria became full-scale in the early 1970s, Japan increased her oil purchases from Nigeria to maximum amounts. Thus while Nigeria's export of oil to Japan amounted to zero in 1970, it was valued at $13 million in 1971 and at $71 million in 1972. Similarly the importance of Zaire to Japan increased due to the existence of reserves in Zaire of various mineral resources. [14]

A third group of countries receiving Japanese aid loans was composed of the relatively more developed nations of Malaysia and Peru. Both of these countries have exported tangible amounts of agricultural, forestry, fishery, and mineral products to Japan. For example the value of timber exports from Malaysia to Japan amounted to more than $210 million in 1972. Malaysia also exported to Japan close to $90 million worth of tin a year, while Peru's exports of minerals and mineral products to Japan amounted to $178 million in 1972. Thus while trade opportunities between Japan and these two countries presented similar cases, Japan's extension of aid loans to each of them differed as a result of the existing political and economic system in each country. As Peru adopted a nationalist socialist approach and nationalized almost all foreign enterprises, Japan provided only token amounts of meaningful aid. To Malaysia, however, Japan has been more willing to extend development loans, since Japanese firms have been permitted to engage in business in Malaysia. As a result the amount of Japanese loans extended to Malaysia was more than twice the amount extended to Peru (see Table 5.9). The grant cost-element of Japanese loans to Malaysia and Peru also reflected this policy. Three loans to Malaysia, one amounting to $50 million and two to $58.5 million, carried a grant cost-element of 36 percent and

TABLE 5.9

Face Value and Grant Cost-Element of
Japanese Aid Loans to Malaysia and Peru

Year	Loan ($ million)	Grant Cost-Element (percent)
Malaysia		
1966	50.0	34.29
1972	58.5	44.59
1972	58.5	34.63
Total	167.0	38.02
Peru		
1971	17.5	50.03
1972	44.1	30.86
1973	12.9	30.86
Total	74.5	35.36

Source: Compiled by the author from
Appendix B.

45 percent, while three loans extended to Peru, amounting in total
face value to $74.5 million, carried an average grant cost-element
of 35 percent. [15]
A fourth group of countries receiving Japanese aid loans consisted of the Far Eastern countries of South Korea and Taiwan. These
countries, unlike Southeast Asian countries, lack ample reserves
of vital mineral and energy resources to trade with Japan. However,
they have been expanding their trade with Japan as they have successfully industrialized their economies with a large inflow of foreign
capital mainly from Japan and the United States. For example their
exports of textiles and machinery to Japan have increased substantially: the value of South Korea's textile exports to Japan increased
from $55 million in 1970 to $120 million in 1972 and Taiwan's textile
exports jumped in value from $33 million in 1970 to $56 million in
1972. Similarly their exports to Japan of machinery increased steadily,
reaching $25 million for South Korea in 1972 and $27 million for
Taiwan. In addition South Korea's exports of fishery products to
Japan jumped from $27 million in 1970 to $71 million in 1972, while
Taiwan's exports of fishery products increased from $25 million in
1970 to $56 million in 1972. In spite of these increased exports to
Japan, both South Korea and Taiwan have continued to suffer from an
unfavorable balance of trade with Japan. While this trade imbalance
has been reduced substantially, in 1972 Japan's exports to South
Korea, $980 million, were still nearly twice the amount of her imports

from South Korea, $426 million. Similarly Japan's exports to Taiwan in 1972 amounted to $1,091 million against her imports of $422 million from Taiwan.[16]

Given this balance of trade in favor of Japan, one would expect a massive flow of Japanese ODA loans at concessional terms to both these countries. Contrary to such an expectation, Japan's official aid to these countries has been limited due to political considerations. South Korea in 1965 received a Japanese loan containing a large cost-element of 46.9 percent (see Table 5.10) as part payment for her establishment of diplomatic relations with Japan, as already noted. South Korea then received no official development loans until 1971, when two loans were extended to her by Japan with a grant cost-element of only 17.5 percent. From 1971 to 1973 Japan extended a number of large loans to South Korea with grant cost-elements ranging between 31 and 47 percent; these were for the modernization of agriculture and fisheries, assistance to medium and small-scale industries, construction of subway lines, commodity purchases, and the expansion of telecommunication networks.[17] When a Korean politician who opposed President Park of South Korea was taken back

TABLE 5.10

Face Value and Grant Cost-Element of
Japanese Aid Loans to South Korea and Taiwan

Year	Loan ($ million)	Grant Cost-Element (percent)
South Korea		
1965	200.0	46.93
1971	20.0	17.52
1971	35.1	17.52
1971	88.4	40.30
1972	25.0	46.93
1972	25.0	30.83
1973	20.0	39.43
Total	413.5	40.40
Taiwan		
1965	50.0	36.64
1965	100.0	24.16
1971	26.2	25.58
Total	176.2	27.91

Source: Compiled by the author from Appendix B.

TABLE 5.11

Face Value and Grant Cost-Element of
Japanese Aid Loans to Brazil and Mexico

Year	Loan ($ million)	Grant Cost-Element (percent)
Brazil		
1962	17.5	20.90
1965	7.7	16.45
1965	24.9	18.76
1966	13.3	18.76
1971	1.9	19.96
1972	178.6	17.05
1973	23.4	15.95
1973	39.0	15.95
1973	16.2	16.35
Total	322.5	17.22
Mexico		
1966	10.0	22.74
1969	8.0	16.50
1969	3.1	14.81
1970	0.5	13.91
1971	2.4	13.80
1971	2.5	14.47
1971	8.9	15.34
1971	7.4	14.47
1972	1.0	14.47
1972	3.0	15.95
1972	0.8	15.34
1973	32.5	15.94
Total	80.1	16.46

Source: Compiled by author from
Appendix B.

to South Korea from Japan in violation of Japanese sovereignty, Japanese aid to South Korea was suspended for an indefinite period of time.

Taiwan also initially received a large loan, in 1965: it amounted to $150 million, with a large grant cost-element, and was part of Japan's effort to undertake katagawari. Taiwan's second loan, however did not come until 1972 when the Export-Import Bank of Japan extended Taiwan a $26.2 million loan. The establishment of diplomatic relations between Tokyo and Peking in September 1972 terminated formal relations between Tokyo and Taipei. As a result part of the funds of the second loan remained unspent. [18]

A fifth group of recipient countries —composed mostly of Latin American countries—represented the most developed among the developing countries aided by Japan. The Japanese government found considerable potential in these countries for increasing Japanese private investments, and viewed the economies of these countries as requiring government incentive but relatively small concessions in terms of aid loans. Reflecting this view, the grant cost-element of loans for both Brazil and Mexico has in fact declined; the first loan to Brazil was extended in 1961 with a grant cost-element of 20.9 percent, and Mexico obtained her initial loan in 1966 with a 22.7 percent grant cost-element. Subsequent loans extended to Brazil in 1973 then carried a grant cost-element of 16 percent and 16.4 percent, while a loan extended to Mexico in 1973 carried a grant cost-element of only 16.0 percent (see Table 5.11).

NOTES

1. Goran Ohlin, Foreign Aid Policies Reconsidered (Paris: OECD Development Center, 1966), annex, pp. 101-105. Appendix C of this study shows how to derive the equations presented in Ohlin's exposition. Wilson Schmidt and Charles Frank have expanded conceptual frameworks for ascertaining the optimal distribution of aid resources and the desirable terms of loans. For the purpose of this study, however, these models provide little additional information to determine the burden to the donor. See Wilson Schmidt, "The Economics of Charity: Loans Versus Grants", Journal of Political Economy, August, 1964, pp. 387-95 and Charles Frank, "Optimal Terms of Foreign Assistance", Journal of Political Economy, September-October, 1970, pp. 1107-1114.

2. Tsusansho, Keizai Koryoku no Genjo to Mondaiten: 1973 (Tokyo: 1973) pp. 146-168.

3. John Pincus, Economic Aid and International Cost Sharing (Baltimore: Johns Hopkins University Press, 1965), p. 134.

4. Ohlin, op. cit., pp. 70-84.

5. OECD, Development Cooperation: 1969 Review (Paris: 1969), p. 290.
6. Martha Loutfi, The Net Cost of Japanese Foreign Aid (New York: Praeger, 1973), pp. 70-71.
7. Tsusansho, Keizai Kyoryoku no Genjo to Mondai-ten 1969, p. 122, 1971, p. 146, and 1973, p. 168.
8. N. H. Jacoby, An Evaluation of the Economic Aid to Free China: 1951-1965 (Washington D. C.: Aid for International Development, 1966).
9. OECD, Development Co-operation: 1973 Review, (Paris: 1973), pp. 138-139.
10. Tsusansho, Keizai Kyoryoku no Genjo to Mondai-ten (1973), p. 386.
11. Tsusansho, Tsusho Hakusho (Kakuron: 1973), pp. 398-406.
12. Ibid., p. 392.
13. Gaimusho, Biruma no Jiryoku Kosei Rosen to Wagakuni no Keizai Kyoryoku (Tokyo, 1972) pp. 151-159.
14. Tsusansho, Tsusho Hakusho, op. cit., pp. 658-62.
15. Ibid., pp. 376-80, 615-19.
16. Ibid., pp. 350-60.
17. Tsusansho, Keizai Kyonyoku no Genjo to Mondai-ten (1973), p. 124.
18. Ibid., p. 317.

As noted previously, Japan developed her industry and overall
economy not only substantially but surprisingly rapidly during the
postwar years from 1945 to 1972. By the end of the 1960s (known
in Japan as the decade for the "income-doubling plan") Japan had
achieved the world's third largest gross national product, and had
become one of the few countries continuously registering a trade
surplus. However, rapid economic expansion based on heavy industrialization caused three major problems. First, as Japan's exports
increased steadily, a trade imbalance emerged in favor of Japan,
creating envy and resentment on the part of many countries trading
with the Japanese. Second, Japan's dependence on relatively few
countries for supplies of energy resources and mineral products increased and became almost a complete dependence. Third, continuous
heavy industrialization led to a deterioration in environmental conditions in Japan, necessitating a reorientation of her national goals
and policies. To deal with these three problems the Japanese government began to redesign its foreign aid program. Kaihatsu yunyu, or
the so-called development-cum-import scheme, was initiated as one
of Japan's new aid measures in the middle of the 1960s. According
to this scheme, the Japanese government was to provide capital and
technical assistance to develop and process natural resources in
recipient countries for their eventual export either to Japan or third
countries. By implementing the scheme Japan hoped not only to secure
vital energy resources and raw materials but to reduce trade imbalances
and environmental deterioration at home.

TRADE IMBALANCES

While Japan's exports remained small, and less than her imports,
until the early 1960s, her exports started expanding steadily in the

78

TABLE 6.1

Japanese Exports and Imports, 1955-72 (million dollars)

Year	Exports	Imports
1955	2,010.6	2,471.4
1956	2,500.6	3,229.7
1957	2,858.0	4,283.6
1958	2,876.6	3,033.1
1959	3,456.5	3,599.5
1960	4,054.5	4,491.1
1961	4,235.6	5,810.4
1962	4,916.2	5,636.5
1963	5,452.1	6,736.3
1964	6,673.2	7,937.5
1965	8,451.7	8,190.0
1966	9,776.4	9,522.7
1967	10,441.6	11,663.1
1968	13,971.7	12,987.2
1969	15,990.0	15,023.5
1970	19,317.7	18,881.2
1971	24,018.9	19,711.7
1972	28,591.1	23,470.7
1973	36,930.0	38,313.6

Source: Tsusansho, Tsusho Hakusho 1972, pp. 362-63, and 1973, pp. 412-13, and 1974, pp. 476-477.

mid-1960s. After that, a trade gap emerged in favor of Japan and slowly began to widen until it was finally reversed in 1973, as shown in Table 6.1.

Japanese exports increased by $1.8 billion in 1965 from the previous year, helping to record Japan's first trade surplus at about $260 million. Since then, the trade surplus has gradually increased to over $430 million in 1970, to more than $4.3 billion in 1971, and to $5.0 billion in 1972.

As Japan stepped up her export drive criticism of Japan as an "economic animal" began to spread in the late 1960s throughout many countries trading with Japan. Various trade imbalances in favor of Japan created frustration and resentment among her trading partners, a factor which in turn strengthened the argument for more Japanese aid. [1]

Against this background the idea of kaikatsu yunyu was put forward, and encouraged, by Tsusansho and other Japanese government ministries. It was considered essential for the developing countries to strengthen their export industries by expanding production and processing of primary products, including those not only in the agricultural sectors but in the mineral, forestry, and fishery sectors as well. Since large-scale expansion of these sectors required extensive improvements in a developing country's infrastructure and social overhead, various aid agencies had to be called upon to provide necessary capital and technical assistance to private firms engaged in the development of import activities. Consequently such agencies as the Export-Import Bank of Japan, the Overseas Economic Cooperation Fund, the Petroleum Development Agency, and the Minera Exploration Agency were asked to modify their rules and regulations for the purpose of guaranteeing and encouraging such "development-cum-import" activities. In addition the Overseas Trade and Development Association was set up in February 1970 in order to reduce imbalances in trade and to facilitate both the development and import of primary products by providing funds for the construction of roads and bridges, hospitals and schools, and other infrastructure and social overhead facilities directly related to the production of primary products. [2]

While the general principle of the "development-cum-import" scheme covered all sectors of the developing countries, and particularly those nations suffering adverse balances of trade with Japan, the scheme was applied in reality to the exploitation of energy and mineral resources.

Before describing the outcome of the "development-cum-import" scheme we will, first, explain Japan's position in energy resource consumption and imports, as well as in mineral resources and renewable resources such as timber. We will then examine the extent of funds provided by Japan to various countries for "development-cum-import" purposes, and finally we will examine the Japanese response to the Arab oil embargo of 1973-74.

Energy Requirements

Energy consumption in Japan increased gradually by about 50 percent from the mid-1950s to 1960s, with total energy consumption reaching the equivalent of 109 million tons of coal in 1960. During the next 10 years energy consumption in Japan more than tripled, amounting to the equivalent of 332 million tons of coal in 1970, as shown in Table 6. 2. Japanese production of energy declined during this 10-year period; the difference between domestic production and consumption was made up by imports from abroad.

The share contributed by each of the energy resources in meeting the aggregate energy demands of Japan has changed over this period of years, as shown in Table 6. 3. In 1955 about half, or 49. 2 percent, of her energy supply came from coal, which Japan possessed in

TABLE 6.2

Energy Consumption and Production in Japan
(million tons of coal equivalent)

Year	Total Consumption	Production
1965	174.59	62.12
1970	331.90	54.88
1971	341.90	49.47

Source: United Nations, Statistical
Yearbook, 1971, p. 338, 1972, p. 355, and
1969, p. 326.

considerable quantity; hydro and nuclear power provided 21.2
percent of the total supply and oil provided 20.2 percent. By 1960
coal declined to a 41.5 percent share of the supply and oil increased
its share to 37.7 percent. While hydro power production increased
by more than 30 percent, its share of the energy supply remained
more or less the same. By the end of the 1960s energy supplies
from oil increased by more than seven times and oil's share climbed
to 68 percent of the total supply. [3]
    While Japanese oil production averaged around 880,000 kiloliters
throughout the last five years of the 1960s, the amount of oil Japan
imported tripled from 1965 to 1972. With her oil imports going from
31 million kiloliters in 1960 to 250 million kiloliters by 1972, this
meant that Japan's dependence on foreign oil amounted to more than
99.5 percent of her supply by 1970 (see Table 6.4).
    Petroleum in fact is not the only commodity for which Japan
depends on foreign countries almost entirely; Japan has been relying

TABLE 6.3

Japanese Energy Supply, by Sources (percentage)

Year	Electric (hydro and nuclear)	Coal	Oil	Others
1955	21.2	39.2	20.2	7.5
1960	15.3	41.5	37.7	5.5
1965	11.3	27.3	58.4	3.0
1968	7.9	23.6	65.6	2.9

Source: Kagaku Gijitsu Cho Shigen Chosa Jo, Nippon no Shigen
Zusetsu (1971), p. 259.

81

TABLE 6.4

Japanese Imports and Production of Petroleum
(1,000 Kiloliters)

Year	Imports	Production
1960	31,131	593
1965	84,143	751
1968	139,830	869
1969	167,428	875
1970	197,108	899
1971	222,490	979
1972	249,193	950*
1973	289,698	1,000*

* Production figures for 1972 and 1973 are estimates.
Source: Japanese prime minister's office, Japan Statistical Yearbook: 1972, pp. 300, 1, 171; Tsusansho, Tsusho Hakusho (Kakuron 1973), p. 287, and Tsusho Hakusho (Kakuron: 1974) p. 267.

on foreign supplies of most of the major mineral products, as shown in Table 6.5. Over the period from 1966 to 1971 Japan's dependence on foreign sources increased from 65.6 percent to 81.9 percent for copper, from 25.6 percent to 67.6 percent for lead, from 96.8 percent to 99.1 percent for iron, and from 59.1 percent to 78.4 percent for coal.

Raw materials and mineral resources are held by a relatively small number of countries. Thus a few countries have often provided more than half of the total mineral imports of Japan. In the case of crude oil, as shown in Table 6.6 more than 70 percent of Japanese oil imports came from Iran, Saudi Arabia and Indonesia in 1973. Also

TABLE 6.5

Percent of Japanese Mineral Supplies Provided from Overseas

Mineral	1966	1971
Copper	65.5	91.9
Lead	25.6	67.6
Iron ore	96.8	99.1
Bauxite	100.0	100.0
Petroleum	99.2	99.6

Source: Keizai Kyoryoku Kikin Shosabu, Kaigai Keizai Kyoryoku Bekkan: 1972, pp. 432-33.

TABLE 6.6

Major Suppliers of Oil to Japan

	1973 Quantity (1,000 kiloliters)	1973 Value ($ million)	1974 Quantity (1,000 kiloliters)	1974 Value ($ million)
Iran	85,589	933	97,253	1,826
Saudi Arabia	29,002	332	68,100	1,285
Indonesia	26,006	318	41,533	1,109
Kuwait	17,060	192	25,784	476
Abu Daabi	—	—	26,686	552
Ohman	5,545	65	7,835	152
Brunei	3	—	9,996	254
Nigeria	—	—	6,005	168
Others	33,903	396	6,507	178
Total	197,108	2,236	289,698	6,000

Source: Tsusansho, Tsusho Hakusho: (Kakuron) 1973, p. 287 and 1974 (Kakuron), p. 267.

83

in that year Canada, the Philippines, Chile, and Australia supplied more than three-fourths of the copper brought into Japan, and imports of iron ore from Australia, India, Brazil, Chile, and Peru counted about 80 percent of the total Japanese import of iron ore. Furthermore in 1972 Australia, Indonesia, and Malaysia alone supplied more than 98 percent of the entire consumption of bauxite in Japan; in the case of rubber, three countries —Thailand, Malaysia, and Indonesia — provided about 90 percent of the total Japanese import in 1973.[4]

As her dependence on relatively few countries for oil supplies deepened, Japan became concerned about the possibility of an almost complete dependence on these countries. She thus consciously endeavored to both diversify her sources of oil supply and maintain cordial ties with her major suppliers.

The concentration of energy and mineral resources in a small number of less-developed countries meant that these resources could be used by supplying nations as possible bargaining tools for political and economic concessions to be made by a foreign resource-dependent donor country like Japan. Natural resources at the same time constituted the only valuable productive factor the less-developed countries had for their own development. As the Japanese became increasingly concerned with their deepening dependence on a few countries for energy resources in particular, they sought to find ways to serve the interests of both Japan and the less-developed countries.

To better ascertain this situation, the government of Japan sent an investigating mission to the Middle East, Europe, and North America in September and October of 1970. Upon its return the group recommended that Japan strengthen her ties with oil-producing countries, following the examples of West Germany and other European countries. Keizai Doyukai, around the same time, proposed that Japanese economic cooperation programs be "organically" tied to energy resource development, taking into account the need in the resource-possessing countries for investment in infrastructure and the improvement of social overhead facilities.[5]

Environmental Deterioration

Rapid, intensive postwar industrialization in Japan meant high intensification of land use for various economic activities, particularly industrial and manufacturing activities. With a national total land area smaller than that of the State of California, Japan's GNP per unit of land in 1970 amounted to well more than four times that of the entire United States; while the GNP of the United States (excluding Alaska) was about $65,000 per square kilometer in 1960, Japan's GNP was already $116,000 per square kilometer. By 1970 the GNP per square kilometer increased to $124,000 in the United

TABLE 6.7

Concentration of Gross National Product, United States and Japan

GNP Concentration	1960	1970
United States		
Total value in $ million	509, 028	969, 574
Unit land value in $ million per sq. km.	65, 000	124, 000
Japan		
Total value in $ million	43, 098	197, 808
Unit land value in $ million per sq. km.	116, 000	533, 000

Source: Japan, Environment Agency, Kankyo Hakusho: 1972, p. 26 (data from OECD, National Accounts and FAO, Production Yearbook, IMF international financial statistics).

States, but the increase in Japan was even more dramatic with the figure climbing to $533, 000, as shown in Table 6.7.

While the concentration of economic activities in European countries has been more intensive than in the United States, it was still less than half that of Japan. In other words one unit of level land in Japan shouldered a burden of sustaining economic activities far more than that of a comparable unit in the European countries and twelve times that of the United States.

Comparison of manufacturing activities in Japan and the United States also shows the high geographical concentration of Japanese industry. While the value of total output in manufacturing has been increasing at the rate of 7 percent to 8 percent per annum in the United States, it has been increasing in Japan at the rate of 14-to-16 percent per annum. In 1969 the value of total output in manufacturing was $658 billion in Japan or five times that in the United States. [6]

The spread of Japanese industry into former farming areas in the vicinity of large cities has substantially reduced the land available for agricultural production, requiring further efforts at land reclamation.

From the point of view of Japan's environmental conditions, the significant aspect of postwar industrialization is that it utilized large amounts of mineral products. As noted above, the consumption of mineral products has been increasing at the rate of 10-to-20 percent a year in Japan. This increased consumption had by 1969 made the consumption of mineral products, per unit of land, eight times higher in Japan than in the United States (see Table 6.8).

Japanese utilization of mineral products in industrial processing was made possible by increased utilization and discharge of water. For the period from 1962 to 1968 alone, the consumption of industrial water in Japan increased from 27 million tons to 36 million tons a day,

TABLE 6.8

Concentration of Mineral Products Consumption
Japan and United States, 1968 (per square kilometer)

Product	Total Consumption Japan	U.S.	Ratio of Consumption per Square Kilometer (Japan/U.S.)
oil	1,028	4,787	4.5
iron ore	51,221	126,187	8.6
copper	785	1,707	9.6
lead	546	1,339	8.6
aluminum	696	3,684	3.9
zinc	546	1,339	8.6

Note: Oil given in million barrels, other products in thousand tons.

Source: Keizai Shingikai Shigen Kenkyu L-inkai, Kokusaika Jidai no Shigen Mondai, 1969, pp. 15, 19, 22, 28, and 36.

representing a 30 percent increase. The major portion of this increase resulted from the use of water for treatment of paper and chemicals and allied products, and for cooling of materials in chemicals and the iron and steel industries. Chemicals were discharged into rivers and bays, polluting them badly within a short period of time.

Industrialization and economic expansion facilitated the process of Japanese urbanization and motorization due mainly to Japan's external economy. A megalopolitan complex emerged, connecting Tokyo, Osaka, and Nagoya with metropolitan areas around Sanyo and Kita Kyushu. Inflows of people into cities caused both an absolute economic expansion and an increase in population density. In Tokyo and Osaka the density reached, respectively, 5,328 and 4,110 persons per square kilometer in 1970.

The number of automobiles in Japan increased astronomically during the 1960s. There were less than one million automobiles in Japan before 1960. The country started producing vehicles on a mass-production basis in the early 1960s, and the number of automobiles steadily increased until it passed 6 million in 1966. Resulting congestion of streets and roads has accentuated some of the density effects of automobiles.

As the result of Japan's rapid and intense industrialization her environmental conditions deteriorated steadily, with the actual effects being felt principally in water and air resources. Water pollution, starting in rivers passing through such major urban centers as Tokyo and Osaka, began to spread into smaller rivers, bays, and surrounding seas by the mid-1960s. Air pollution also spread from Japanese metro-

politan areas to suburbs and then to the countryside as the result of
the emission of sulfur oxides, nitrogen oxides, and other pollutants
discharged by thermal power stations, industrial plants, and automobiles. The most conspicuous water pollution is currently found in rivers
which go through large metropolitan areas, particularly Tokyo, Osaka,
Fukuoka, and Nagoya. The water quality of many of the rivers is
even today lower than the minimum standard set by the Japanese
government. A second water pollution problem is the eutrophication
of lakes and marshes. As the result of growths of algae that feed on
nitrogen and other nutrients contained in fertilizers and other wastes,
many lakes are filled with weeds. The frequency of outbreaks of algae
odor in some lakes, like Lake Biwa, has been increasing. A third
problem is the diversification of pollutants and particular forms of
contamination. In the mid-1960s hydrogen concentration, chemical
oxygen demand, and suspended solids were the only substances of
major concern; but in the 1970s, pollutants found in rivers, lakes,
and bays have included waste oil, copper, zinc, iron, calcium,
mercury, lead, and organic phosphorus. All of these pollutants have
made impossible the use of water not only for drinking and other home
purposes but for fishing and irrigation purposes.

The development of petrochemical, steel, and other manufacturing
and processing plants, which expanded rapidly as the result of Japan's
postwar industrialization policy, discharged sulfur oxides, nitrogen
oxides, and other pollutants causing serious air pollution. Atmospheric
pollution was further worsened by the emission of pollutants from
thermal power stations and automobiles. While the Japanese government claims that the major toxic pollutants reached their maximum
level in 1969, subsequent monitoring of the level of oxidants and
other pollutants in the air has not confirmed clear decline in the
overall level of polution in Japan since 1969. Instead, there have
recently been a number of photochemical smogs in Japan, in some
cases causing widespread severe eye irritation, eye drips, sore
throat, coughing, and even serious difficulty in breathing. [7]

Japanese concern over environmental problems (kogai mondai)
has developed slowly. The first major incident that triggered widespread concern was a Minamata disease outbreak in Japan in the
mid-1950s, which received considerable publicity for several months.
However, as few causal factors in the outbreak were clarified, public
concern began to fade away in the midst of controversy over the
renewal of the U. S. -Japan security treaty. A second Minamata outbreak, in 1964, resulted in a more acute awareness on the part of
the Japanese public as scientific findings following the outbreak
illuminated the actual nature of kogai mondai. Methyl mercury was
reported to be the cause of the disease, but it was found to be discharged from fertilizer plants. The Minamata disease, according to
experts, occurred when people in Minamata Village and Niigate

prefecture ate fish that had accumulated methyl mercury compounds discharged by fertilizer plants. Another disease, called Itai-itai disease and resulting from chronic cadmium, soon followed, killing more than 30 persons.

The government of Japan at first took palliative measures to minimize the adverse effects of pollution on human health. However, as environmental deterioration progressed, it became the most embarrassing issue faced by the government before opposition political parties and at international conferences. Thus after spending several years enacting regulatory measures the government finally began to consider the possibility of reducing pollution by changing national priorities. New economic and social development plans were then issued and revised three times between 1969 and 1973. [8]

The basic Japanese commercial and industrial policy for the 1970s was formulated in 1971 by the Industrial Structure Deliberation Committee in 1971. The committee, consisting of 35 members from government, business, and academic communities, met 40 times; it spent almost two years deliberating before submitting a report in June 1972. [9] It recommended in its report that Japan's industrial structure be changed from one based on heavy petrochemical industry to an information-centered industrial base. Concerning economic development cooperation, the committee recommended that Japan adopt the following aid policies:

1. facilitate economic cooperation from the point of view of aid-receiving countries but without being bound to the direct interest of Japan

2. open Japan's market to products made in developing countries and establish rational international division of labor

3. formulate economic cooperation policies suited to the special situation of each developing country and implement these policies efficiently

4. utilize willingly foreign exchange and other means available to expand and strengthen economic cooperation.

In addition to urging these specific measures to be taken by the Japanese government, the committee recommended that Japan encourage the development of overseas natural and energy resources and the processing of primary and mineral products.

The central theme of the committee's recommendations was that Japan had reached the point where she would have to turn from heavy industrialization utilizing enormous amounts of energy and mineral resources to information and high-technology industries requiring mainly high-level technical know-how. Such a transformation of Japanese economic structure would, in the committee's view, serve to attain five fundamental objectives in the 1970s (1) strengthen the overall potentiality of industry and the foundation for development; (2) improve the quality of living conditions; (3) secure desirable social and environmental conditions and build a more beautiful land; (4) expand worthwhile jobs and establish safe and enjoyable working conditions; and (5) promote leadership for the harmonious development of both the Japanese economy and the international economic community. [10]

Outcome of "Development-cum-Import" Scheme

The "development-cum-import" scheme (kaihatsu yunyu), as mentioned previously, was originally aimed at reducing excessive trade imbalances favorable to Japan, securing for Japan adequate supplies of raw materials and energy resources, and reducing environmental deterioration in Japan. These three objectives were intertwined; most of Japan's aid projects were designed to aim not only at one objective but at the others at the same time. The importance of the three objectives, however, differed according to their proximity to the basic national goals of Japan, survival and ascendancy. The extent of actual capital and technical assistance provided indicates that the highest priority was accorded to those programs that aimed at meeting immediate needs for Japan's survival, namely, supplies of basic raw materials and energy resources. Only secondary attention was given to the other two objectives as the effects of both environmental problems and trade imbalances in favor of Japan were less direct and immediate than shortages of energy and primary products. As a result the bulk of Japanese aid resources was increasingly directed to countries with rich natural resources, particularly oil. Resource-poor nations among the less-developed countries tended to be neglected as being of secondary importance.

The kaihatsu yunyu scheme was originally conceived of as a means of remedying Japan's trade surplus with certain aid recipient countries and, at the same time, to secure agricultural and other primary products by helping these countries develop their natural resources. This "convenient" view turned out to be only partially applicable to the actual world economic situation. Countries that had been suffering chronic unfavorable trade balances with Japan were not necessarily countries with rich natural resources. As shown in Table 6.9, 13 Asian countries had unfavorable balances of trade with Japan in the three years from 1970 through 1972—South Korea, Hong Kong, Taiwan, Cambodia, South Vietnam, Thailand, Singapore, Burma, Bangladesh, Sri Lanka, Laos, Afghanistan and Nepal. Of these countries only one, Burma, had ample reserves of energy and mineral resources possibly sufficient to change the direction of the generally unfavorable balance of trade; the other countries had relatively little to offer of what Japan most needed.

Countries that had vital natural resources needed by the Japanese economy were Malaysia, the Philippines, Iran, Indonesia, India, and

TABLE 6. 9

Trade Imbalances in Favor of Japan ($ million)

Trading Country	1970	1971	1972
South Korea	798. 2	571. 3	535. 8
Hong Kong	608. 5	689. 3	790. 3
Taiwan	449. 7	642. 3	448. 8
Cambodia	4. 8	9. 6	9. 3
South Vietnam	141. 5	145. 2	90. 8
Thailand	259. 6	215. 2	270. 1
Singapore	236. 5	394. 1	580. 6
Burma	26. 2	41. 2	20. 2
Bangladesh	—	—	37. 8
Sri Lanka	7. 6	15. 5	5. 8
Laos	6. 6	6. 2	3. 3
Afghanistan	21. 4	20. 3	32. 4
Nepal	3. 7	4. 0	6. 6

Source: Tsusansho, Tsusho Hakusho (Kakuron 1973), pp. 346-47.

Brunei (in Asia), the Arab countries in the Middle East, Zambia and Nigeria (in Africa), and Brazil, Peru, and Chile (in Latin America). And, as shown in Table 6. 10, these were among the countries that were enjoying favorable balances in their trade with Japan.

The fact that the Japanese government aimed at securing adequate supplies of energy and other natural resources from less-developed countries through the use of foreign aid is seen in the lending practices employed by the Export-Import Bank of Japan. In its extension of loans made directly to foreign governments and corporations, the Export-Import Bank of Japan has made conscious efforts in favor of less-developed countries. From 1958, when its first loan was extended to India, to the end of March 1971, the Bank provided $823 million to Southeast Asia, $97 million to East Asia, $104 million to Latin America, $14 million to West Asia, and $13 million to Africa; over the same period it extended only $4 million to Europe and no funds at all to North America. [11]

The credit policy of the bank was further adjusted to help meet Japan's basic objective (steady supplies of energy and other natural resources). The Bank increased its credit extension for natural resource development projects, under its export, import, and overseas investment credit programs. In the fiscal year 1972 credit commitments for this purpose totaled 187. 6 billion yen ($60 million), representing an increase of 42 percent from the 1971 figure of 132. 1 billion yen ($37 million). The major natural resource development projects

90

consisted of the import of enriched uranium amounting to 99.1 billion yen ($32 million) and an oil resources development project with a cost of 74.8 billion yen ($24 million). As shown in Table 6.11, these two items alone represented 95 percent of the entire commitment for natural resource development projects.

The increasing importance placed on natural resources exploitation and on manufacturing activities is clearly seen in the distribution of Japanese private investments in less-developed countries. As shown in Table 6.12, the total cumulative value of Japanese private investment in these countries amounted to $3,217 million as of March 1973. Two-thirds of the entire investment was in the manufacturing and mining sectors, while the remaining one-third was divided among such other sectors as commerce, construction, banking and insurance, agriculture, forestry, and fishery.

The investment in the manufacturing sector totaled $1,292 million. Almost all of it went to Asia and Latin America, Asia receiving $720 million and Latin America $496 million; by comparison, other areas received only $76 million. The investment in the mining sector

TABLE 6.10

Japanese Trade Imbalances in Favor of Various Trading Countries
($ million)

Trading Country	1970	1972
Malaysia	252.4	131.5
Philippines	80.7	23.0
Indonesia	320.8	582.0
India	186.9	167.8
Pakistan	96.0	46.9
Brunei	9.3	85.9
Iran	816.6	1,108.0
Saudi Arabia	342.3	673.4
Kuwait	213.9	432.0
Abu Dahbi	0.0	129.0
Ohman	62.6	121.8
Mexico	57.3	51.1
Peru	157.5	114.5
Chile	181.0	147.5
Brazil	51.2	145.9
Nigeria	50.1	56.0
Uganda	22.1	17.3
Zambia	262.9	119.6
Ghana	3.7	33.5

Source: Tsusansho, Tsusho Hakusho (Kakuron 1973), pp. 346-47, 420-21, 584-85.

TABLE 6.11

Credit Commitment of Japanese Export-Import Bank
for Natural Resources Acquisition (billion yen)

Resource	Fiscal 1971	Fiscal 1972
Iron ore	16.4	2.8
Copper, copper ore	6.9	2.8
Uranium	1.6	99.1
Other metal	14.1	—
Oil	76.9	74.8
Coal	1.4	6.7
Lumber and pulp	13.8	1.4
Others	2.1	0.1
Total	132.1	187.6

Source: Japan, Export-Import Bank, Annual Report: March 1972–
March 1973, p. 15.

TABLE 6.12

Japanese Private Investments in Less-Developed Countries
as of March 1973 (million dollars)

Sector	Manufacturing	Mining	Others	Total
Latin America	496.0	164.8	328.4	989.2
Asia	719.9	371.4	298.4	1,389.7
Middle East	7.4	376.8	222.2	606.4
Africa	32.2	85.0	30.8	148.0
Oceania	22.9	32.1	11.3	66.3
Europe	13.5	—	3.9	17.4
Total	1,291.9	1,030.0	895.0	3,216.9

Note: "Others" are agriculture, forestry, fishery, construction,
commerce, banking and insurance.
Source: Tsusansho, Keizai Kyoryoku no Genjo to Mondai-ten
(1973), p. 174.

totaled $1,030 million. Reflecting the new investment trend, the Middle East and Asia received the largest amounts, $377 million and $371 million respectively. Latin America and Africa also absorbed substantial amounts of Japanese private investments in mining, respectively $165 million and $85 million.

Effects of Arab Oil Embargo

The oil crisis of late 1973 and early 1974 revealed Japan's readiness to place the highest priority on the utilization of her foreign aid program for securing the energy resources that constituted an essential prerequisite for Japan's survival. As the only means available to Japan, both Japanese capital and technology were offered, in lieu of military arms, in return for restored oil supplies from the Middle East.

When the Arab oil ministers met on October 17, 1973 in Vienna, they decided to increase the amount of the oil embargo by 10 percent each month in those countries which were not considered as "friendly" countries. Japan was chosen as one of the countries subject to this further oil cut. The Arabs then demanded that to be designated a "friendly" country and thus avoid the cutbacks Japan would have to break off her diplomatic relations with Israel, extend military aid to Arab countries, and stop trading with Israel. These measures proved to be too severe for the Japanese to accept. Instead, the Japanese offered to increase their economic aid and private investment going to the oil producers. Japan then pledged to increase her contributions to U.N. aid to Palestinian refugees from $1 million in 1973 to $5 million in 1974. [12] Japan also declared that she supported Resolution 242 of the U.N. Security Council, which urged Israel to withdraw from Arab territories occupied during the war of 1967. However, such a policy statement was considered insufficient by the Arabs. The Japanese government then indicated that if Israel did not withdraw from Arab territories, Japan might have to "reconsider its policy toward Israel"; this policy statement was still considered weak and insuffi- by the Arabs. [13] The Arab envoys that visited Tokyo in December 1973 insisted that to reverse any cutbacks in oil supply Japan would have to take three steps: persuade Israel to withdraw from all of the Arab territories she occupied; urge the United States to compel Israel to accept a Middle East settlement on terms satisfactory to the Arabs; and expand substantially Japanese economic aid to Arab countries. [14]

The Tanaka government then sent Deputy Premier Takeo Miki to various Arab countries to "explain" Japan's policy on the Middle East issue, to obtain the "understanding" of the Arabs on the Japanese policy, and to ascertain what Japan could do to contribute to peace in the region. It became apparent, however, that Japan had developed almost no policy on the Middle East issue and as such could do almost nothing to contribute to peace in the region; all she could do in fact was offer economic and technical aid. Consequently the Japanese government pledged in late 1973 and early 1974 a number of aid packages to oil producers and their allies. (As a result the allocation of Japanese aid was expected to change drastically after 1974.) These aid pledges included a $140 million loan to Egypt for the restoration and expansion of the Suez Canal; a $23 million loan for refinery construction in Syria; $1 billion for Iraq for various industrial projects; and $1.5 billion for Iran for refinery and petrochemical plant construction.

This change in Japan's position was not as great as the Arabs had hoped for. It was, however, a gain considered more tangible than any others the Arabs received. Consequently when the Arab oil ministers met again on December 25, 1973 in Kuwait, they issued a statement declaring a reduction in oil cutbacks to Japan, thereby assuring Japan's existing oil needs:

> The ministers' meeting in Kuwait noted the changes in the Japanese policy vis-a-vis the Arab cause, which was conveyed through various ways and means, one of them the visit paid by the Vice Premier of Japan to some of the Arab countries, and on the other hand they noted the economic situation of Japan, and therefore decided to treat especially Japan in a way which does not subject that country to the general reduction as a whole, doing this in order to protect the Japanese economy and hoping that the Japanese Government would appreciate this position and continue to take fair and equitable positions for the Arab cause. [15]

NOTES

1. Osamu Shimomura Keizai Taikoku Nippon no Sentaku (Tokyo: Toyo Keizai Shimposha, 1972), pp. 592-610.

2. Gaimusho, Keizai Kyoryoku no Genjo to Mondai-ten (1972), p. 256.

3. Japan, Environment Agency, Air Pollution Control in Japan, May 1972, p. 2.

4. Tsusansho, Tsusho Hakusho Kakuron (1974), p. 231, 234, 251, 252 and 267.

5. Tsusansho, Keizaikyoryohu no Genjo to Mondaiten (1971), pp. 112-113.

6. United Nations, Statistical Yearbook: 1970, pp. 225-26; and Japan, prime minister's office, Japan Statistical Yearbook: 1969, p. 646.

7. Japan, Environment Agency, op. cit., pp. 15-16; and Asahi Shimbun, April 22, 1973.

8. Asahi Shimbun, February 9, 1973.

9. Sangyo Kozo Shingi Kai, 70 nen dai no Tsusho Sangyo Seisaku: Interim Report (May 1971).

10. Tsusansho, Keizai Kyoryoku no Genjo to Mondai-ten (1967), pp. 137-140; and Kazuo Saito, "Nippon no Nogyo Kyoryoku no Atarashii Arikata," Sekai Keizai Hyoron, September 1970, pp. 37-42.

11. Export-Import Bank of Japan, Export-Import Bank of Japan: Its Role and Functions (June 1971) p. 36.

12. Tetsushi Okakura, "Nippon no Chuto Shin Seisaku was Minoru ka," Economisto, December 4, 1973, pp. 18-22.

13. New York Times, December 1, 1973.

14. New York Times, December 11, 1973.

15. New York Times, December 26, 1973.

JAPANESE POLICIES
TOWARD MULTILATERAL
AID AGENCIES
AND PROGRAMS

Japan regarded her participation in multilateral assistance organizations and programs, first, as an effort to realize her reentry into kokusai shakai, or the international community, and, second, as a means of rising in the community by securing her leadership position (see Chapter 1). In this chapter we will examine how Japan actually participated in various multilateral aid agencies and programs, both regional and global, noting which of these organizations Japan joined or initiated. We will then discuss Japan's degree of success in her attempts to move up not only in the regional community but also in the global community.

LEGITIMIZATION OF JAPAN'S POSITION
IN INTERNATIONAL COMMUNITY

To secure her position as a member of the international community, Japan first applied for admission to the United Nations, this coming immediately after the end of Allied occupation of Japan in June 1975.[1] Japan's application for U. N. membership, however, was not taken up for several years, until December 1956. It became a cold war issue in the era of East-West confrontation. Thus, unable to establish her membership position in the global organization, Japan sought to legitimize her position by (1) participating in the Colombo Plan and (2) joining certain subsidiary organs of the United Nations. The Colombo Plan provided Japan with her first opportunity to demonstrate her willingness to contribute to international cooperation programs in consultation with other countries. At the same time Japan's membership in the U. N. Economic Commission for Asia and the Far East (ECAFE) and in various specialized U. N. agencies qualified her as a member of the global community. Her subsequent attainment of membership in the Development Assistance Committee (DAC) and in the committee's overall body, the Organization for Economic Cooperation and Development (OECD) in 1964 meant that Japan was now regarded as a member of what was known as the "rich nations' club".

The Colombo Plan was established by the British Commonwealth of Nations foreign ministers in 1950 for the purpose of coordinating economic and technical assistance activities undertaken in the Commonwealth countries. The plan had two features. First, it was designed as a consultative organ for its members, and, second, it was not an implementing agency, neither collecting nor disbursing any funds of its own. Participating countries merely met annually to formulate a coordinated plan for separate implementation by each member. As the effectiveness of the Colombo Plan became widely appreciated, countries outside the Commonwealth began to join the plan when its door became open to them. For Japan the plan presented a forum well suited for her own objective of becoming a member of a regional setup without being heavily bound either politically or financially.

Since joining the plan in 1954, Japan has provided economic and technical experts and has accepted foreign trainees and students in consultation with plan members. The trainees and students that received training through the Colombo Plan numbered 69, 604 for the period from 1950 to 1970, with an additional 7, 395 receiving training in 1971 and 5, 229 in 1972. Japan accepted a total of 6, 216 trainees and students for the period from 1950 to 1970, an additional 1, 087 in 1971, and 998 in 1972. Japan's role in sending economic and technical experts to various countries also increased over this period; from 1950 to 1970 Japan provided 2, 079 experts, or about 15 percent of the total number of experts provided, 14, 135, under the Colombo Plan as a whole. In 1971 and 1972 the number of Japanese experts provided totaled, respectively, 589 and 658, constituting about half of tne plan's total number of experts, 1, 178 and 1, 469, provided in those years. [2]

As it became clear that Japan's membership could not be readily accepted by the United Nations, even wnen Japan regained her sovereignty, she sought to join ECAFE, a subsidiary regional organ of the U. N. Economic and Social Council. After a long period of debate Japan was voted into ECAFE in 1954. [3]

In 1951 Japan applied for membership in various specialized agencies of the United Nations, and during the next two years she was accepted by each of these bodies: the World Health Organization (WHO), the International Labor Organization (ILO), the U. N. Educational, Scientific, and Cultural Organization (UNESCO), and the Food and Agricultural Organization (FAO).

Once Japan had been accepted as a member of these U. N. agencies she cast few dissenting votes, faithfully following the rules and regulations of the organization, and paid her dues and fees regularly on time. Such efforts to act as a model member, along with a lessening of the Soviet Union's opposition to Japan as the result of normalized diplomatic relations between the two countries, resulted in the admission of Japan to the United Nations in December 1956.

Japan further pursued her policy of joining the groups of advanced nations of Western Europe and North America. For example when the Organization for European Economic Cooperation (OEEC) set up a Development Assistance Group (DAG) in 1960, Japan was certified as a member of the group. By then Japan was regarded as a donor of aid on the basis of her participation in the Colombo Plan and her disbursement of aid resources through reparations payments. DAG became the Development Assistance Committee (DAC) in the following year when the OEEC was reorganized as the Organization for Economic Cooperation and Development (OECD). Both DAG and DAC represented an exclusive club of the principal donor countries. They held consultations on the general principles and policy issues concerning development assistance, and conducted inquiries into the aid programs of each of their members. The only actual requirement placed upon members was the submission of reports on aid performance in conformity with uniform reporting criteria. A few years later, in April 1964, Japan became a formal member of OECD. As Olson noted:

> Joining OECD had great symbolic importance: it signified formal acceptance in the "club of rich nations", Japan was the only non-Western nation in the club. It also assuaged a fear of isolation that had persisted in Tokyo ever since the European Economic Community was organized, when the United States appeared intent upon closer European ties. It ensured that Japan would be a party to all discussions of aid and balance-of-payments problems among the "have" nations. [4]

Japan had thus seemed successful in using cooperative activities, through the Colombo Plan and subsidiary organs and agencies of the United Nations, for the purpose of attaining one of her current national goals, the establishment of Japan's position not only in the regional community but in the global community. Japan had also established herself as a member of the group of developed Western countries.

Japan's Position in Regional Cooperation Activities

In addition to the global United Nations and OECD, there are a number of regional cooperation programs that have been set up for various purposes —military, political, economic, functional, and sociocultural. Some programs and institutions were set up early in existence for a number of years. Others are relatively new, having been in existence for only a few years. The regional institutions and programs also have varying membership with different political, social, economic and cultural backgrounds. In this section, we shall ascertain the extent of Japan's participation in and her contributions to these institutions and programs by asking the following question: Did Japan participate in and contribute to not only economic but military and political organizations for the sake of realizing ascendancy? For the purpose of this examination, we first identify major regional coopera- tive institutions, agencies, programs and groups which were created since World War II. They are listed in Table 7. 1.

Military Alliances

Regional organizations in Asia set up for military purposes are SEATO and CENTO. Both of these groups were created in the 1950s, through U. N. initiative, for the purpose of counteracting Communist forces. SEATO has eight members —the United States, Australia, the Philippines, Thailand, New Zealand, the United Kingdom, France and Pakistan. Members of CENTO include five nations—Iran, Iraq, Pakis- tan, Turkey, and the United Kingdom, with the United States as an observer. Japan has refrained from participation in either of these treaty organizations. Japan has in fact avoided any military associa- tion with foreign countries other than with the United States.

Political Associations

The extent of Japan's participation in regional political organiza- tions and programs has been somewhat limited. Of all the organiza- tions and programs set up in Asia, only three may be regarded as primarily political: the Asian and Pacific Council (ASPAC), the Asian Parliamentarians' Union (APU), and the Association of Southeast Asian Nations (ASEAN). While Japan participated in ASPAC and in APU, she did not become a member of ASEAN.

ASPAC was established in 1966 for the explicit purpose of facil- itating an exchange of views among its members on political, economic, social, and cultural matters and to promote their cooperative activities in each field. The primary objective of the council, however, turned out to be political; from the beginning such members of the council as South Korea, the Philippines, and South Vietnam saw the need to con- centrate their consultations on the defense of the Asian region against Communist threats. While Japan joined ASPAC under the Sato govern- ment in 1966, Japan and Malaysia remained hesitant during the strong anti-Communist deliberations held at council meetings. At the

TABLE 7.1

Regional International Organizations in Asia

1947   Economic Commission for Asia and the Far East (ECAFE)
1950   Colombo Plan for Cooperative Economic Development in South
        and Southeast Asia
1954   South East Asia Treaty Organization (SEATO)
1957   Committee for the Coordination of Investigations of the Lower
        Mekong Basin (Mekong Development Committee)
1957   Central Bank Conference of South East Asia, Australia and
        New Zealand (SEANZA)
1958   Eastern Regional Organization for Public Administration (EROPA)
1959   Central Treaty Organization (CENTO)
1961   Asian Productivity Organization (APO)
1961   Asia and Far East Institute for the Prevention of Crime and
        Treatment of Offenders (UNAFEI)
1961   The Asia Electronic Conference
1961   Association of Southeast Asian Nations (ASEAN)
1963   International Institute of Seismology and Earthquake Engineering
        (IISEE)
1964   Asian Institute for Economic Development and Planning (AIEDP)
1965   Asian Parliamentarians' Union (APU)
1965   Asian Development Bank (AsDB)
1965   Southeast Asian Ministers of Education Organization (SEAMEO)
1966   Ministerial Conference for the Economic Development of
        Southeast Asia (MCEDSA)
1966   Asian and Pacific Countil (ASPAC)
1966   Southeast Asian Central Bank Group
1967   The Coordination Committee of Southeast Asian Senior Officials
        on Transport and Communication
1967   The Cultural and Social Center for Asia and Pacific Region
1967   Asian Institute of Technology
1969   Food and Fertilizer Technology Center for Asian and Pacific
        Region
1969   Asian Coconut Community (ACC)
1970   Asian Statistical Institute (ASI)

Source: Gaimusho Ajiya Chi-iki Kyoryoku Kenkyu Kai, *Ajiya no Chi-iki
        Kyoryoku Kiko* (Tokyo: 1971).

council's second meeting in 1967, six members—the Philippines, South Korea, South Vietnam, New Zealand, Australia, and Thailand— indicated their active support of the efforts of the United States and South Vietnam in the Vietnam War. Fearful of any possible involvement in the Vietnam conflict, Japan advocated that ASPAC give more consideration to economic and cultural matters than to political affairs. As the East-West confrontation came to an end following the establishment of rapprochement between the United States and China in 1972, ASPAC was the first organization to lose its raison d'etre and subsequently dissolve. In 1973 the council adjourned for an indefinite period of time as Malaysia refrained from sending her delegation to a council meeting and other members of ASPAC also lost interest in the council's activities.[5]

ASEAN was established in 1961 by Indonesia, Malaysia, Singapore, and the Philippines to maintain the neutrality of Asian subregional areas. ASEAN has gained due recognition from the international community, having been the first attempt by the subregional countries of Asia to undertake consultations without help from external powers. Along with other nations outside the subregion, Japan was excluded from membership in ASEAN. As ASEAN has concentrated its efforts on subregional cooperative programs, it has not only survived but has strengthened its position over the years.

APU was proposed by Japan in 1965 for nominally political consultations among members of various representative bodies from the participating countries. The union consists of participants from South Korea, Japan, Malaysia, the Philippines, and Indonesia. While the group has distinctively non-Communist characteristics, it has maintained a low profile without particularly stressing any single ideological line.

While ASPAC, ASEAN, and APU are the only Asian groups that directly serve political purposes, the other organizations and programs in Asia may be said to be playing roles within a broad framework drawn by political and ideological factors. A breakdown of the memberships of 17 major Asian regional organizations and programs is given in Table 7.2; it shows that those regional institutions in which Japan participates also tend to include Indonesia, Malaysia, the Philippines, South Korea, South Vietnam, and Thailand. As noted in Chapter 5, these are also the countries favored the most by Japan in the extension of her aid resources.

Economic and Social Activities

Most of the regional assistance activities and programs in Asia are in various economic and social fields. They have been set up as a result of initiatives taken jointly by a group of countries in the

101

TABLE 7. 2

Member Nations in Regional Organizations and Programs in Asia

Member Nation	1	2	3	4	5	6	7	8	9	10	11	12	13	14	15	16	17
Afghanistan	x	x										x				x	
Australia	x	x	x	x	x						x	x				x	
British Solomon Islands	x																
Brunei	x																
Burma	x	x										x					
China	x																
Fiji	x											x					
Hong Kong	x		x	x								x				x	
India	x	x	x	x	x							x				x	
Indonesia	x	x	x	x	x		x	x	x			x	x		x	x	x
Iran	x	x	x	x	x	x	x									x	
Japan	x	x	x	x	x	x		x		x	x	x		x	x		
Khmer Republic	x	x	x						x			x		x	x		
Laos	x	x	x			x		x	x	x		x				x	x
Malaysia	x	x	x		x			x	x	x		x	x	x	x	x	x
Maldive Islands	x	x															
Mongolia	x																
Nauru	x																
Nepal	x	x				x						x				x	
New Zealand	x	x	x	x							x	x				x	
Pakistan	x	x	x	x	x	x		x				x				x	
Papua and New Guinea	x											x					
Philippines	x	x	x	x	x	x		x	x	x	x	x	x	x	x	x	x
South Korea	x	x	x		x	x		x			x	x				x	
South Vietnam	x	x	x	x	x		x	x	x	x	x	x		x		x	x
Singapore	x	x			x			x	x	x		x	x	x		x	x
Sri Lanka	x	x	x		x							x			x	x	
Thailand	x	x	x	x	x	x		x	x	x	x	x	x	x	x	x	x
Tonga	x											x				x	
Western Samoa	x											x					
Taiwan				x	x	x					x	x					

Note: 1—ECAFE; 2—Colombo Plan; 3—SEANZA; 4—Mekong Committee; 5—EROPA; 6—Asian Productivity Organization (APO); 7—Regional Cooperation and Development (RCD); 8—APU; 9—SEAMEO; 10—MCEDSA; 11—ASPAC; 12—ADB; 13—ASEAN; 14—Southeast Asian Senior Fisheries Development Center (SEAFDEC); 15—ACC; 16—ASI; 17—Southeast Asia Trade, Investment, and Tourism Promotion Center (SEATITC).

Source: Kajima Heiwa Kenkyujo, Taigai Keizdi Kyoryoku Taikei, vol. 8 (Tokyo: Kajima Kenkyujo Shuppankai, 1973), pp. 13-27.

102

United Nations or individually by an influential country such as the United States or Japan. By far the largest number of programs and organizations have been established under the auspices of ECAFE. ECAFE represents Asia's most important regional organization, including the participation of almost all of the Asian countries. During the early part of the postwar era Japan's participation in regional programs as limited to such existing noncontroversial agencies and programs as the Colombo Plan, ECAFE, and the Mekong project. At first Japan acted cautiously in all of these groups, but as she became a dominant economic power in Asia by the middle of the 1960s, she started not only to increase her contributions to existing regional cooperation programs but to take various initiatives in establishing both the Asian Development Bank and the Ministerial Conference for the Economic Development of Southeast Asia (which later became major lending and consultative bodies).

Mekong Committee

Following the adoption by ECAFE of recommendations from a U. S. Bureau of Reclamation study undertaken in 1956 for the development of the Lower Mekong River basin in Southeast Asia, the Mekong's four bordering countries of Cambodia, Laos, Thailand, and South Vietnam set up the Committee for Coordination of Investigations of the Lower Mekong Basin, later to be commonly called the Mekong Development Committee. Basically the committee's work was to oversee the planning and execution of water resources development projects in the Lower Mekong basin. In spite of recurrent fighting in the Mekong region, these development projects have grown in number and complexity, acquiring total operational resources of $ 270 million by the end of 1973.

Overall, the Mekong project was characterized by three developments: First, the program was initially promoted by the United States and France. Second, Japan later joined in the Mekong project and gradually became a major supporter of it. Third, Western supporters of the project, particularly the United States, began to feel threatened by new world influences being exerted by China, the USSR, and Japan.

The project was launched through three studies conducted to provide a basis for the design of a regional development program for the Lower Mekong basin. The first of these studies, done at the request of ECAFE in 1951, investigated the general problems and opportunities created by international rivers in Asia. The Mekong was then selected for specific study in terms of its engineering possibilities. And finally, following the Geneva accords of 1954, which brought a temporary halt to fighting in the Mekong area and the separation of North and South Vietnam, both France and the United States encouraged those states bordering on the Mekong to undertake a reconnaissance study of the area. Such a study was completed, and a report containing the results of the study was endorsed by ECAFE in 1957. As a result the four Mekong region countries agreed to set up the abovementioned coordinating committee under ECAFE's guidance.

The specific functions of the Mekong Committee were (1) to prepare and submit to the participating governments a plan for coordinated investigation and study of the Mekong basin; (2) to make requests on behalf of the participating governments for special financial and technical assistance, and to receive and administer separately such financial and technical assistance as may be offered under the technical assistance program of the United Nations, its specialized agencies, and friendly governments; and (3) to draw up and recommend to participating governments various criteria for the use of water from the main Mekong river for the purpose of water resource development.

When the Mekong Committee started its planning and coordination work, the United States contributed the largest amount to the Mekong activities. American contributions to preinvestment investigations and planning came to nearly one-third of the total—$22.2 million out of the total of $71.7 million. The United States provided a proportionally less amount of funds for actual investment, $22.1 million out of a total of $153.3 million. [6]

To the United States, the multilateral Mekong activities meant not only simple economic cooperation but also a counterbalance to other growing influences being exerted by China, the USSR and Japan. A staff report to the subcommittee on National Security Policy and Scientific Developments of the Committee on Foreign Affairs of the U.S. House of Representatives was explicit in noting the strategic importance of the Mekong project:

U.S. policy toward the Mekong Project can be approached in a number of ways. First, it can be regarded as an element of U.S. national security policy in the sense that it is a move toward building a more unified regional complex of countries as a counterbalance to Mainland China and the presence of USSR in Asia, as well as to a revitalized Japan. Second, it can be regarded as a point of departure toward a limitless variety of forms of economic assistance to a developing region; also, as a mechanism for shifting multilateral arrangements with more sharing of costs among the developed countries (and a "lower profile" of each individual donor). Third, as a very long range diplomatic strategy, the concept of "world regionalism" perhaps offers a way to restructure national political forces into economically balanced regions, sharing interests and problems, but with lessened levels of interregional conflict and tensions while building viable

regional systems of economic and technological development, interregional trade, and mutual assistance. [7]

Japan, joining the Mekong Committee in December 1958 proposed
to undertake a part of the overall Mekong scheme, the aforementioned
reconnaissance survey of the major tributaries of the Mekong basin,
and to contribute $ 240, 000 toward the cost of undertaking such a
survey. Reflecting Japan's current national policy, which emphasized
the importance of overseas economic expansion, her main objective
in participating in the Mekong project was to open up a new area for
entry by Japanese firms. As in many other cases, an informal study
group was set up in Tokyo consisting of business leaders and government officials. Familiar names in this group included those of Ataru
Kobayashi, president of Arabian Oil, Yutaka Kubota, president of
Nippon Koei, and Saburo Okita, who was responsible for the "income-
doubling plan" (discussed previously) and who later became president
of the Overseas Economic Cooperation Fund (OECF).

The Mekong tributaries reconnaissance survey was launched in
1958. A number of Japanese construction and power companies, government agencies, and trading companies sent representatives to accom-
pany the survey team. Kubota headed the survey, which produced a
major reference report for further work to be undertaken by the Mekong
Committee. Following the survey Japan's involvement in the Mekong
project increased steadily; for example Japanese firms drew up designs
for a dam in northeastern Thailand and supervised its construction.

As Japanese influence increased, a feeling of uneasiness grew
among other world leaders involved in the Mekong project. As Olson
noted, they felt "as though there might be well-laid plans for a new
co-prosperity sphere built around exploitation of regional resources. "[8]
The Japanese, meanwhile, seemed to feel that they were being kept
around the periphery of international development planning; no Japanese
representative was found among the top decision makers of the secretariat assisting the Mekong Committee. [9]

Japan's financial contribution to the Mekong project increased
steadily after she joined, and she became the second largest contributor among non-Committee members by 1972 (see Table 7. 3). By the
end of 1973, Japan's contribution to operational resources amounted
to close to $30 million.

Asian Development Bank (ADB)

By the time the creation of the Asian Development Bank had been
formally proposed at a meeting of ECAFE in 1963, Japanese political
and business leaders had completed their consultations and drawn up
their proposals regarding the bank. They visualized Japan's role in

TABLE 7.3

Total Contributions to Mekong Project, as of December 31, 1972

Contributor	Amount ($ million)
Non-committee members	
United States	44, 349, 858
Japan	17, 751, 588
West Germany	17, 554, 412
Netherlands	6, 971, 023
France	6, 879, 360
Australia	3, 744, 458
Others	
Subtotal	112, 884, 641
Committee members	
Khmer Republic	12, 840, 233
Laos	4, 306, 406
Thailand	62, 799, 530
Vietnam	13, 834, 517
Subtotal	93, 669, 686
International agencies	17, 740, 043
Private foundations	691, 494
Grand Total	224, 985, 964

Source: Mekong Committee, Annual Report: 1972, p. 145.

the bank as being similar to the role played by the United States in the World Bank. The headquarters of the bank was to be located in Tokyo and a Japanese to be appointed as its president. However, the Japanese underestimated the uneasiness of other Asians toward such a plan placing the bank entirely under Japanese control. This pressure resulted in the board's decision to designate Manila as the location for the bank's headquarters. The movement of voters is shown below:[10]

First Voting		Second Voting		Third Voting	
Tokyo	8	Tokyo	8	Manila	9
Teheran	4	Manila	6	Tokyo	8
Manila	3	Teheran	4	absention	1
Kuala Lumpur	1				
Singapore	1				
Total	18		18		18

Japan did succeed, however, in securing the post of the bank's presidency for a Japanese national. In addition Japan helped launch the bank, in 1965, with a capital subscription amounting to $200 million, or about 20 percent of the bank's total capital, $1, 005.4

million. Japan and the United States, which subscribed an equal amount of capital, were the bank's leaders. During the next several years Japan gradually emerged as the most important member of the bank as it attempted to expand its scope of lending activities and capital in the early 1970s. The bank proposed to set up special funds —for agricultural programs, technical assistance, and multipurpose activities—to be built from voluntary contributions. Japan made available a total of more than $230 million, or more than 2/3 of the amount of the special funds (see Table 7.4). As of December 1973, total contributions to the special funds amounted to $343 million. In addition to Japan a major contributor was India, which provided more than $27 million for agricultural funds.

TABLE 7.4

Total Voluntary Contributions to Special Funds of
Asian Development Bank as of December 1973 ($ thousand dollars)

Contributor	Technical Assistance	Multi-purpose Funds
Australia	779	12,949
Austria	112	
Canada	200	27,057
Taiwan	200	
Denmark	756	2,385
Finland	116	1,599
West Germany	367	25,095
India	241	
Italy	200	1,699
Japan	8,118	226,429
South Korea	30	
Netherland	199	8,964
New Zealand	396	1,176
Norway		2,095
Pakistan	24	
Sri Lanka	20	
Switzerland	200	6,173
United Kingdom	482	13,859
United States	1,250	
Total	13,690	329,480

Note: The amount equivalent to $27.1 million was contributed by Denmark, Japan and Netherlands for the Agricultural Special Fund. These contributions, however, were repaid or reallocated for other purposes when the Fund was cancelled in May 1973.
Source: Asian Development Bank, annual report: 1973, pp. 80-81.

TABLE 7.5

Total Capital Subscriptions by Major Members of
Asian Development Bank, as of March 1973 (million dollars)

Member Country	Amount Subscribed	Member Country	Amount Subscribed
Regional		Nonregional	
Japan	603	United States	241
Australia	256	W. Germany	103
India	280	United Kingdom	90
Philippines	106	Canada	75
Pakistan	97	France	75
South Korea	139	Italy	24
Indonesia	75	Austria	15
Malaysia	60	Belgium	15
Thailand	60	Denmark	15
Taiwan	48	Switzerland	15
Others	280	Others	53
Total	2,004	Total	721

Source: Tsusansho, Keizai Kyoryoku no Genjo to Mondai-ten
(1973), p. 515.

As shown in Table 7.5, regional members of the bank responded
affirmatively to this decision by pledging new subscriptions; as a
result the amount of subscriptions by the regional members now
totaled 1,595.7 million. Most of the Western European members
also responded positively, with capital subscribed by the bank's
nonregional members increasing from $380 million to $581 million;
the United States did not increase her share. In fact the amount of
subscriptions from Australia and India now surpassed that of the
United States. Japan's subscription amounted to $500 million, con-
stituting by far the largest share among both regional and nonregional
members.

In the management of the bank Japan has also exerted considerable
influence in the decision-making process as her nationals have occupied not only the bank's presidency but several principal posts in the
operations, projects, and treasury departments of the bank. In 1972,
among the 36 principal officers, seven were Japanese; two out of
seven operations managers and two out of seven projects managers
were Japanese; and a Japanese occupied the post of deputy treasurer.[11]

Ministerial Conference for Economic Development
of Southeast Asia

By the middle of the 1960s the Japanese became confident that
Japan had successfully established her position in the Asian regional
community through her participation in ECAFE, the Colombo Plan, and
the Mekong project. They felt further that with the economic strength
Japan was rapidly acquiring she could set up, under her leadership,
a consultative group on economic cooperation with the rest of Asian
countries. The Sato government thus embarked upon the formation of
the Ministerial Conference for the Economic Development of Southeast
Asia; Indonesia, the Khmer Republic, Laos, Malaysia, the Philippines,
Singapore, Thailand, and South Vietnam responded to Japan's efforts
by attending the first session of the conference in Tokyo in 1966.

The Japanese government aimed at attaining three objectives
through the ministerial conference. First, it wanted to promote the
conference as a forum for explaining Japanese aid policy; second, it
hoped to lay the basis for Japan's major role in the reconstruction of
Indo-China after the Vietnam War; and third, it aimed at consolidating
its leadership position in Southeast Asia and paving the path for
Japan's overall ascendancy in Asia.

Conscious of the sensitivity of other Asian countries to any
revival of Japan's prewar Daitowa Kyoei-ken, Japan encouraged participants in the conference to propose various ideas and programs.
Out of these proposals a number of cooperative activities emerged;
the most notable were the Coordination Committee of Southeast Asian
Senior Officials on Transport and Communication (1967), the Southeast
Asian Senior Fisheries Development Center (1967), and the Southeast
Asia Trade, Investment, and Tourism Promotion Center (1972). Japan
carefully reviewed the conference's various proposals and promoted
those activities that she saw as enhancing her own kokueki. Such a
self-centered approach drew criticism from a few countries regarding
the real motives behind Japan's efforts. [12] In spite of the criticism
the ministerial conference proved to be a viable ongoing institution
when Australia, Burma, and New Zealand decided to join in the conference in 1973.

The above examination of the outcome of Japan's aid strategy
in regional cooperative activities shows that Japan was successful
in, first, establishing her participation in these various activities
and, then, consolidating her leadership role in the Asian community
consisting mainly of non-Communist countries. Japan in short achieved
ascendancy in Asia. We will examine below Japan's policies toward
global multilateral assistance agencies and programs. This will be
done in terms of Japan's participation in the World Bank and in the
U. N. Development Program.

Japan's Approach Toward Global Aid Agencies and Programs

Global assistance agencies differ significantly from regional
arrangements in several ways. First, the number of members of global
groups is usually three to four times larger than that of regional
institutions; second, there are several major donor countries in the
global agencies, while Japan tends to be the only country in the
Asian region that could make substantial contributions to any regional
cooperative program; third, the global agencies formulate their policies
on a global scale; and fourth, Japan is a relative newcomer to many of
the global agencies. All of these conditions require a country like
Japan to contribute relatively more financially should she wish to
exercise any effective leadership in the activities of global agencies.
Furthermore, since the global agencies would tend to be less geared
to provide tangible and direct benefits to Japan in return for her financial contribution to them, the extent of Japanese contributions to
global agencies should be a good indicator of the extent of Japan's
willingness to define its role in the global community.

Embryonic Force in the World Bank

As the U.N. Relief and Rehabilitation Administration struggled
to meet urgent relief and rehabilitation requirements in war-torn
countries at the close of World War II, it soon became apparent that
assistance had to be provided not only to the devastated nations but
also to newly emerging countries that were poor and underdeveloped.
Foreseeing such a need, the Allied powers met in Bretton Woods,
N.H. in July 1944 to find a solution to the aid problem. The outcome
of this conference was the establishment of both the International
Monetary Fund (IMF) and the International Bank for Reconstruction
and Development (IBRD), or World Bank, as it was later to be commonly called.

According to the agreement concluded at Bretton Woods, the
World Bank was to allocate its resources "exclusively for the benefit
of members with equitable consideration to projects for development
and projects for reconstruction alike."[13] It was noted in Article 1,
Section 1 of the agreement that the bank was "to assist in the reconstruction and development of territories of members by facilitating
the investment of capital for productive purposes . . . and the
encouragement of the development of productive facilities and resources in less-developed countries." The other major objectives
of the pact were outlined (in Article 1, Sections 2-4) as the promotion
of private foreign investment, the realization of the long-range balanced growth of international trade, the maintenance of equilibrium

f balances of payments by encouraging international investment, and
he achieving of a smooth transition from a wartime to a peacetime
economy.

While setting forth these objectives, the participants in the conference tailored the role of the bank to supplement the existing international financial system. Henry Morgenthau, Jr., who was president
of the conference as well as the head of the U.S. delegation, noted
hat the main function of the World Bank was "to guarantee private
loans made through the usual investment channels." Because the
bank was to make loans only when these could not be extended through
normal investment channels, "the effect would be to provide capital
for those who need it at lower interest rates than in the past and to
drive only the usurious money lender from the temple of international
finance."[14] The World Bank was thus created under the firm leadership of the United States, according to U.S. understanding of the
existing problems and proposed solutions.

The creation of the World Bank had three significant implications:
t was viewed as a purely capitalist scheme by the Soviet bloc; it
was regarded by less-developed countries as an institution of advanced Western powers designed to help the developed nations and
not necessarily the poor countries; and it was considered an institution in which the defeated powers of the war, such as Germany and
Japan, had no voice in its creation and little participation in its
management and operation.

When the agreement establishing the bank came into effect in
December 1945, the Soviet Union did not join the bank even though
it had participated in the Bretton Woods Conference. Several other
Communist countries, which did participate in the initial period of
he bank's operation, withdrew later. Poland left the Bank in 1950,
Czechoslovakia in 1954, and Cuba in 1960. For these countries the
bank represented an attempt by Western capitalist countries to perpet-
uate their economic domination of the world.

Representatives of less-developed countries attending the Bretton
Woods Conference showed their misgivings about the fact that most
of the bank's resources would be allocated for reconstruction projects
and relatively little for development. They demanded that the bank
make equal amounts of funds available for both reconstruction and
development purposes. Lord Keynes, of Great Britain, argued against
his demand, saying that it would make the bank unable to allocate
more funds for development purposes after reconstruction was completed.[15] The U.N. delegation at the conference also did not have
any intention of making the bank an institution designed solely to
help finance development projects in underdeveloped countries.

The misgivings of the less-developed countries were justified as
he bank started operations; until early 1949 the bank extended no
significant loans to underdeveloped countries. The total amount of
loans made by the bank for development purposes amounted to no more

111

than $100 million. [16] Thus disappointment in the underdeveloped countries was deep, but these countries had little means at their disposal to change the policy of the bank. The bank was set up as an international financial institution managed by major shareholders in the same manner as in any traditional capitalist institution. Furthermore the bank advocated the application of sound banking policies to the recipient governments. The bank thoroughly reviewed its development program, its debt service capacity, and its feasibility of new projects before undertaking any lending. To maintain such principles of sound banking and be able to borrow capital from private sources in developed countries, the bank maintained until 1964 an interest rate of 1.25 percentage points above the estimated cost of borrowing. [17]

As recent enemies, Germany and Japan were left out of the bank at the time of its establishment; Japan, however, was to benefit from the operations of the bank for many years to come. Japan joined the World Bank in August 1952 shortly after she regained her sovereignty. The bank then extended two loans, totaling about $40 million, to private Japanese electric companies under the guarantee of the Japanese government. [18] The bank subsequently extended to Japan a number of loans for reconstruction and development purposes. As late as 1964 the bank approved a large loan to Japan amounting to $125 million. The Bank in fact extended loans to Japan up to 1967, finding that Japan continually met the basic criteria for lending. The bank preferred to lend to countries that (1) were creditworthy on bank terms; (2) could not obtain loans at reasonable terms in the private capital market; and (3) pursued policies that ensured their future creditability and contributions to the financing of bank-supported projects. Japan was found to be ideal for meeting these criteria. Only in 1967, when it became clear that Japan would be freely able to obtain loans in private markets, did the World Bank cease to extend her loans. [19] The major recipients of loans and credits from both the World Bank and its affiliated organ the International Development Association are listed in Table 7.6. Japan received more loans than Pakistan, Yugoslavia, and several other nations not listed in the table. The only countries that received more loans than Japan were India, Brazil, Mexico, Pakistan, Iran, Colombia, and Yugoslavia.

While Japan was one of the largest recipients of loans from the World Bank, she remained during the 1960s a relatively minor participant in the management of the Bank. Only in the 1970s has she become one of the major subscribers of the bank's capital, and despite this Japan has not carried as much weight in the bank's operations as she did in the Asian Development Bank.

In 1961 the share of votes held by Japan in the World Bank was 3.17 percent of the bank's total votes. While Japan's absolute number of votes increased substantially over the next ten years, the share of both Japan's capital subscription and her votes increased only margin-

TABLE 7. 6

Major Recipients of Loans from World Bank and
nternational Development Association as of June 1974 (million dollars)

Recipient	IBRD Loans	IDA Loans	Total
India	1, 327. 6	2, 810. 6	4, 138. 2
Brazil	1, 890. 2		1, 890. 2
Mexico	1, 860. 1		1, 860. 1
Pakistan	695. 1	557. 2	1, 252. 3
Iran	1, 158. 2		1, 158. 2
Colombia	1, 128. 3	19. 5	1, 147. 8
Yugoslavia	879. 1		879. 1
Japan	862. 9		862. 9

Source: World Bank, Annual Report: 1974, Appendix 2, pp. 136-39.

ally during the same period and was 3. 92 percent in 1971. As shown
in Table 7. 7, Japan's share of votes then went down to 3. 70 two
years later in 1974 as the share's other member countries —particularly
smaller ones —increased.

In 1974 four other countries held more votes in the bank than
Japan: The United States had the largest share of votes, 22. 94
percent, followed by the United Kingdom, 9. 27 percent; West Germany,
4. 31 percent; and France, 4. 60 percent. Thus while Japan was fifth
in terms of voting power, her share voting was less than one-sixth
of that of the United States and less than half that of the United
Kingdom. That both of these countries held dominant positions in
the bank is also confirmed by the distribution of the bank's professional staff.

The percentage of Japanese nationals on the professional staff
of the World Bank remained small until the 1970s. The professional
staff increased gradually from 180 in 1950 to 254 in 1959 and to 484
in 1965. It then reached 700 in 1958 and expanded to 1, 348 in 1971.
As shown in Table 7. 8, Americans and Britons made up the major
portion of the bank's professional staff over this period although
their percentage of the total staff declined from 71 percent to 42
percent. In 1951 there were 96 Americans and 17 British out of the
total number of 159 professionals; in 1971 there were 370 Americans
and 198 Britons. In contrast to this there was no Japanese citizen
on the professional staff until 1959, and in 1968 there were still
only five Japanese. However, as Japan's capital subscription and her
role in lending to the bank increased rapidly after 1970, the bank
made special efforts to recruit Japanese professionals; the result
was a jump in the number of Japanese professionals to 23 by 1971.

TABLE 7.7

Shares of Votes Held by Various Members of World Bank
(in percentage)

Country	June 1961	June 1971	June 1973
United States	29.25	23.83	22.94
United Kingdom	12.04	9.81	9.27
West Germany	4.93	5.19	4.91
France	4.93	4.02	4.60
Japan	3.17	3.92	3.70
India	3.79	3.46	3.27
Canada	3.56	3.05	3.41
Taiwan	3.56	2.90	2.74
Italy	1.77	2.58	2.44
Belgium	2.18	2.17	2.05
Others	30.82	39.07	40.67
Total	100.00	100.00	100.00

Source: Edward S. Mason and Robert E. Asher, The World Bank Since Bretton Woods (Washington D.C.: Brookings Institution, 1973), pp. 800-02; and World Bank, Annual Report: 1973, pp. 110-11.

TABLE 7.8

Nationality Breakdown of World Bank's Professional Personnel

Nation	1950	1959	1965	1968	1971
United States	115	119	177	220	370
United Kingdom	23	34	83	133	198
Netherlands	9	15	26	35	54
France	6	16	34	44	88
Germany	—	3	24	40	77
India	1	5	13	34	59
Canada	8	10	14	21	50
Belgium	1	3	12	14	25
Japan	—	1	3	5	23
Australia	1	2	7	9	22
Others	1	2	7	9	22
Total	180	254	484	705	1,348

Source: Edward S. Mason and Robert E. Asher, The World Bank Since Bretton Woods (Washington, D.C.: Brookings Institution, 1973), pp. 879-880.

The number of Japanese working in the bank, however, remained still small in comparison with those of other countries.

Otsukiai for United Nations Development Efforts

The extent of Japan's financial contributions and staff involvement in assistance programs sponsored under U. N. auspices has remained relatively small and at the minimum level required of her under otsukiai (see Chapter 1). By far the largest U. N. aid program, extending its coverage to all areas of the world in a systematic manner, is the United Nations Development Program (UNDP). The UNDP was established in January 1966 by consolidation of the EPTA and the Special Fund.

The significance of examining the extent of contributions made to the UNDP lies in the nature of the program. The UNDP represents an embryonic state for a global agency for resource redistribution. Three characteristic features of this embryonic state for such a global agency are, first, UNDP's participant countries are the most universal in number of any development assistance agency with such a magnitude of financing responsibility; second, the decision-making procedure used by UNDP permits a majority voting power for the overall world population, yet allows the advanced countries to decide on the magnitude of their contributions (all of the participants are expected to, and do, contribute to the program in the form of grants); and finally, the distribution of UNDP funds is determined by rational criteria, namely, the size of the population and the level of per capita income of the recipient countries. [20] Since the UNDP constituted an embryonic institution for sekai kyodotai, or a future welfare state as envisaged by Myrdal (see Chapter 2), Japan's actual contribution to the program may be regarded as a tangible indication of Japan's support of the rational approach toward a world community.

Since 1966 when the UNDP launched its operations, Japanese voluntary contributions to the program have steadily increased at the annual growth rate of 20-30 percent. The amount of Japan's contribution more than tripled in seven years; it went from $3 million in 1966 to $10 million in 1973. It increased by a further 40 percent to reach $14 million in 1974 (see Table 7.9). The extent of this increase is thus impressive when Japan's contribution is viewed alone, without any comparison with that of other donor countries.

During the 1960s Japan's marginal contribution to the UNDP reflected the fact that Japan in that period favored the providing of aid through bilateral, rather than multilateral, channels. In the 1970s, however, Japan's contribution to the UNDP began to increase substantially in terms of both its absolute amount and relative share. Two factors seem to have contributed to this rapid increase. First,

TABLE 7.9

Japan's Contributions to U.S. Development Program (thousand dollars)

Year	Contribution	Amount of Increase	Percent of Increase
1966	3,000	—	
1967	3,650	650	22
1968	4,000	350	9
1969	4,800	800	20
1970	4,800	—	—
1971	5,760	960	20
1972	8,000	2,240	37
1973	10,000	2,000	25
1974	14,000	4,000	40

Note: Japan pledged additional $1.5 million for 1973 and $2 million for 1974, for the least developed countries.

Source: UNDP Pre-Investment News, and UNDP Business Bulletin.

Japan began to draw criticism not only from the recipient countries but also from other donor countries. The recipient countries voiced their frustration and anger over the fact that Japanese aid, as directed bilaterally, aimed at serving only the interest of Japan, and not those of the recipient countries. At the same time the Development Assistance Committee of OECD, as noted in Chapter 3, conveyed the concern of other donor countries that Japan was not providing adequate amounts of aid either bilaterally or multilaterally. In time Japan, more conscious of her nouveau riche status, responded to demands that she contribute her "share" to the multilateral assistance programs, according to the concept of Japan's responsibility as a leading member of the international community.

Second, as noted in Chapter 6, Japan's favorable balance of trade continued to widen as she pressed her industrialization and export drives through the early 1970s. As a result Japan's official reserves of gold and foreign exchange deposits, increased steadily in the 1960s and rapidly during the beginning of the 1970s. In 1960 the amount of gold and foreign exchange held by Japan was less than $2 billion, as shown in Table 7.10. This figure increased gradually to $4.4 billion in 1970, and then shot up to $15 billion in 1971, to $18 billion in 1972, and to a record high of $19 billion in February 1973.

Conscious of Japan's embarassing financial position, the Japanese government decided in October 1972 to increase the Japanese contribution to international aid agencies for the purpose of reducing any further

116

TABLE 7.10

Gold and Foreign Exchange Reserves of Japan
(million dollars)

Year	Reserves
1960	1,824
1961	1,486
1962	1,841
1963	1,878
1964	1,999
1965	2,107
1966	2,074
1967	2,005
1968	2,891
1969	3,496
1970	4,399
1971	15,235
1972	18,365
1973 (February)	19,067

Source: The Bank of Japan, Economic
Statistics Annual: 1973 (March 1974), p. 207.

TABLE 7.11

Major Contributors to UNDP (thousand dollars)

Contributor	1970	1972	1974
United States	86,268	86,000	90,000
Sweden	21,000	26,000	36,364
Denmark	15,600	21,302	32,749
Netherlands	9,444	13,750	27,816
West Germany	11,202	15,094	24,384
United Kingdom	15,160	19,927	21,938
Canada	15,000	18,000	22,371
Japan	4,800	8,000	14,000
Norway	5,950	7,862	12,820
France	4,324	5,924	10,000
Others	37,565	46,960	63,823
Total	226,313	268,819	356,265

Source: UNDP Pre-Investment News (November 1971 and 1973)
and UNDP Business Bulletin (December 1974).

excessive increase in her accumulation of foreign reserves. [21] Half
a year later, in February 1973, the Tanaka government adopted a
formal national policy of effecting substantial increases in Japan's
contribution to these international organizations. [22] In spite of these
policy declarations, her position as a contributor to the UNDP improved only marginally in comparison with other major contributors;
in 1970 Japan was ninth in the ranks of the largest contributors. Whil
the amount of Japan's contribution was more than doubled during the
next few years, this placed her only eighth on the list in 1973 as she
surpassed Norway (see Table 7. 11).

Measured in terms of per capita contributions of the donor countries, Japan's performance appeared even more discouraging. While
in 1972 Denmark gave UNDP $4. 19 per capita, Sweden provided
$3. 23 per capita, and the United States $0. 42, Japan contributed
only $0. 08 per capita. In other words one Japanese citizen contribute
to UNDP less than one-fiftieth of a Dane's contribution and one-fifth
of the amount provided by an American. In view of the relatively high
per capita income in the Scandinavian and North European countries,
these countries may be said to have had greater ability to contribute;
the difference between their contributions and those of the Japanese,
however, remains strikingly large.

Japanese participation in the management of UNDP operations, as
noted above, also remains minor; in 1974 there was not a single Japanese person occupying a principal post or other top-level posts in
UNDP. Nor were there more than a few Japanese professionals working
in the UNDP secretariat, in 1974. Lack of active participation in UND
seems to have resulted from both a Japanese conviction that it is an
entity which they could little influence and certain sociocultural factors that made it difficult to effect a smooth entry of Japanese into
the international community (Chapter 8 will examine such sociocultura
factors).

NOTES

1. Japan, Ministry of Foreign Affairs, Japan in the United Nations
(1969) p. 1.
2. Tsusansho, Keizai Kyoryoku no Genjo to Mondai-ten (1973),
pp. 554-56.
3. United Nations, ECOSOC Res. 517 A(XVLL), April 22, 1954.
The U. N. headquarters in New York, however, voiced its objection,
stating that the ultimate decision on membership should be decided
by the General Assembly in New York. Debate on the legality of
Japan's qualifications lasted for about two years before the Economic
and Social Council voted for Japan's full membership in ECAFE.

4. Lawrence Olson, Japan in Postwar Asia (New York: Praeger, 1970), p. 142. Olson noted that Japan was admitted to full membership in 1963. While the invitation to join was issued to Japan by OECD in July 1963, formal entry to OECD was not possible until April 1954 due to delays in ratification of the Invitation by the Japanese Diet.

5. Kojima Heiwa Kenkyujo, Taiigai Keizai Kyoryoku Taikei vol. 8 Ajiya ni Okeru Chi-iki Koryoku, vol. 8 (Tokyo: Kajima Heiwa Kenkyuro, 1973), p. 158.

6. Committee for the Coordination of Investigations of the Lower Mekong Basin, Annual Report: 1972, (E/CN. 11/WRD/MKG/L. 358), p. 105.

7. Franklin P. Huddle, The Mekong Project: Opportunities and Problems of Regionalism, report prepared for the Subcommittee on National Security Policy and Scientific Developments of the Committee on Foreign Affairs, U. S. House of Representatives, May 1972, p. 61.

8. Olson, op. cit., p. 222.

9. Interview held by the author with a Japanese officer who worked on the project. For the staffing situation of the principal posts, see Committee for the Coordination of Investigation of the Lower Mekong Basin, op. cit.

10. Takeshi Watanabe, Ajiya Kaigin Sosai Nikki (Tokyo: Nippon Keizai Shimbun Sha, 1973), pp. 9-13.

11. Asian Development Bank, Annual Report: 1972 (March 1973), pp. 126-127.

12. Asahi Shimbun, October 12, 1973. Admitting such a past tendency to place Japan's interest first, Japanese Prime Minister Tanaka pledged to participants of the conference Japan's willingness to put the welfare of the people in the recipient countries first in the future.

13. Agreement on IBRD: Constitution, Article III-1 (a).

14. U. S. Department of State, Bulletin, vol. 2, July 30, 1944, p. 113.

15. Antonin Basch, "International Bank for Reconstruction and Development, 1944-1949," International Conciliation, November 1949, no. 455, p. 794.

16. Robert E. Asher, Walter M. Kotschning, and William A. Brown, Jr. et al., The United Nations and Economic and Social Co-operation (Washington, D. C.; The Brookings Institution, 1957), p. 318.

17. Edward S. Mason and Robert E. Asher, The World Bank Since Bretton Woods (Washington, D. C.: Brookings Institution, 1973), p. 211.

18. Ibid., pp. 500-501.

19. Ibid., pp. 232-33.

20. United Nations, Report of the Governing Council, Economic and Social Council Official Records: Fifty-Seventh Session, supplement no. 2 (E/5466).

21. Tsusansho, <u>Keizai Kyoryoku no Genjo to Mondai-ten</u> (1972), p. 118.

22. Japan, Economic Planning Agency, <u>Basic Economic and Social Plan: 1973-1977</u> (February 1973), pp. 80-81.

8

The Japanese government, as noted in Chapter 2, claims that Japan has provided technical assistance to developing nations in the belief that she could be effective in transferring the technical know-how she has successfully employed in her own modernization efforts. Such a conviction was reiterated in a statement made by Gaimsho in 1967:

> Japan, whose technical skills and ability are now given worldwide recognition and which has undergone a very rapid reconstruction of its economy with remarkable progress in the field of industrial technique, is naturally expected to do its utmost to strengthen technical assistance. Japan is well aware that it is in the most responsible and suitable position to assist the developing countries through this kind of cooperation. [1]

Despite such a notable statement made several years ago, the Japanese government had to admit in 1973 that "technical cooperation accounts for a very small share of Japan's assistance and significant expansion is required in this area."[2] This chapter will discuss the nature and problems of Japan's technical assistance program, in the light of its wider and more lasting implications for Japan's future cooperative ventures.

In the 1950s Japanese technical assistance activities were confined to training foreigners in Japan and sending Japanese experts in various fields to less-developed countries. But then Japan started sending development survey missions to developing countries and setting up overseas technical cooperation centers to provide training in various fields. In 1964 Japan agreed to supply equipment as part of her technical assistance program, and in 1965, the Japan Overseas Cooperation Volunteers program was established to engage Japanese

121

youths in development activities in a manner similar to that of the U.S. Peace Corps. The scope of the Japanese program continued to expand with the establishment of an assistance plan for both medical and science education in 1966 and the establishment of plans for agricultural development assistance and primary products development assistance in 1967.

Despite these varied programs Japanese technical assistance operations have encountered a number of problems related to language barriers and to significant social and cultural differences between Japan and the recipient countries.

TRAINING PROGRAM IN JAPAN

Training provided in Japan has usually been arranged by the Overseas Technical Cooperation Agency (OTCA), and consists of either group or individual training. For group training OTCA has developed standardized programs that are adjusted to meet the particular requirements of the trainee groups selected from various developing countries. For individual training arrangements are made for individuals from developing countries to come to Japan and receive training on an ad hoc basis at various Japanese technical institutions and government centers, colleges and universities, and private business establishments.

As cited in Chapter 4, the number of various technical trainees and students coming to Japan as part of Japanese technical assistance has remained small in comparison with those received by other donor countries. Japan has received such a relatively small number of students and trainees not only because of her government policy favoring capital lending but also because of limited facilities available in Japan; there are both inadequate physical facilities for accommodating foreign students and little room for these foreigners to enter the Japanese social structure. Furthermore Japan has only a few professionals who are in a position to teach technical matters relevant to the foreign students' requirements in their home countries and who are at the same time qualified to teach in English. Comparatively few Japanese professionals have been acquainted with technical and social conditions prevailing in the countries from which students and trainees come, and an even smaller number of Japanese have mastered English, or for that matter French, to a significant degree.

OTCA has maintained international training centers in five different cities of Japan. These centers are designed to both house the foreigners and hold various seminars and courses. While the centers have been expanded over time, they are still not large enough to receive more than a limited number of foreigners; in 1971 the five training centers together had the capacity to accommodate a total number of 544 trainees and students. The international center in Tokyo handled 291 of these, the Nagoya center handled 100, the Osaka center 70, the Uchihara center 54, and the Misaki center only 29.[3] Whereas students and trainees may find private accommodations relatively easily, and may be invited to many social gatherings, in such other assistance-providing countries as the United States, they have found limited private housing and social opportunities in Japan. In fact most of them have been isloated in Japanese public living quarters, and have resented such treatment.[4]

Language barriers have constituted a major obstacle to the implementation of training activities in Japan. The Japanese language, unlike English, French, or even German, is not widely used or understood outside Japan. In the 1970s the Japanese government began to support the teaching of Japanese in assistance-receiving countries by providing these countries with Japanese language teachers and audio-visual equipment. This approach, however, has had limited success due to the difficulty of learning a sufficient amount of Japanese in a short period of time and the limited use that Japanese has for the students and trainees once they have returned to their own countries.

Japanese Experts Abroad

The first assignments sending various Japanese experts abroad were carried out in 1955 shortly after Japan joined the Colombo Plan. Since then the assignment of technical assistance experts to developing nations has expanded as Japan initiated her own technical assistance program for the Middle East and Africa in 1958 and a similar program for Taiwan in 1960. However, during the course of its expansion the Japanese expert advisory program has encountered a number of administrative, social, and cultural problems that have worked against successful implementation of the program.

Since the commencement of technical assistance in 1955, the cumulative number of various experts sent abroad by Japan grew steadily to reach 5,983 as of December 31, 1971, but more than one-third of these experts were sent out in 1971 alone. As shown in Table 8.1 a total number of 2,978 Japanese experts were reportedly engaged in development activities in 1971; of these more than two-thirds were technical advisers and one-fifth were teachers and other volunteers. In 1972 the total number of experts sent out by Japan reached 3,588, representing an increase of some 20 percent.

The largest number of Japanese experts abroad have represented national government ministries: 162 such experts in 1970, or 34 percent of the total. An additional 112 experts, or 23.5 percent of the total, came from private business firms in 1970, while public

TABLE 8.1

Cumulative Number of Japanese Technical Experts Sent Abroad

Personnel	1971	1972
Educational experts	70	54
Teachers	65	54
Advisers	5	—
Technical advisers	2, 228	2, 799
Volunteers	680	735
Teachers	97	119
Others	583	616
Total	2, 978	3, 588

Source: OECD, Development Co-operation: 1973 Review, pp. 199-201.

TABLE 8.2

Japanese Technical Assistance Experts
according to Employer, 1970

Employer	Number of Experts	Percent of Experts
National ministries	162	34.0
Local government	37	7.8
Public corporations, agencies	70	14.7
Trade assiciations	18	3.8
Private business firms	112	23.5
Universities, research institutions	18	3.8
Self-employed	5	1.1
Mushoku (unemployed)	26	5.5
Blue-collar industries	6	1.3
Former experts	14	2.9
Others	8	1.7
Total	476	100.0

Source: Kaigai Gijutsu Kyoryoku Jigyodan, Gijutsu Kyoryoku Nenpo: 1971, p. 94.

corporations and agencies sent out 70 experts, or 14. 7 percent of the total (see Table 8. 2).

The functions of Japanese technical experts have ranged from advisory service to training and research activities. Initially the group of experts represented only the fields of agriculture, fisheries, construction, and light manufacturing, but by the beginning of the 1960s these had been expanded to include experts from mining, education, telecommunications, health and welfare, administration, and transportation (see Table 8. 3).

Japanese experts seeking to work in overseas technical assistance have encountered certain problems arising out of administrative formalities set down by their employers. There were initially almost no administrative rules allowing long absences on the part of government officers and professionals from their posts. Nor did any concept of technical consulting actually exist in Japanese business. Private companies guaranteed lifetime employment to their personnel but demanded total allegiance from them. With a general unwillingness on the part of employers to release their employees, a number of technical experts had either to sacrifice considerable pay or to wait until retirement if they wished to take even a brief overseas assignment. In 1970, for example, 26 experts had to take overseas assignments as "leave without pay" or after their retirement from former positions. [5]

Not only have there been these domestic difficulties, but frequently experts arriving in various nations to carry out their assignments have been confronted, initially, with language problems and, then, with the problem of not comprehending local customs and traditions. Often this has resulted in disappointment, frustration, and even resentment toward each other for Japanese experts abroad. [6]

Integrated Technical Assistance

Until the middle of the 1960s Japanese technical assistance as carried out through the training of foreigners in Japan and the assignment of experts abroad individually upon the receipt of requests for assistance from recipient countries. There had been little cohesive integration with other requirements of particular nations that needed comprehensive assistance; thus in 1966 and 1967 the Japanese government embarked on a new program of technical cooperation designed to meet the requirements of recipients in a more comprehensive manner. The new program included, plans for overseas assistance in the fields of (1) health and medicine;(2) science education; (3) agriculture and (4) primary products development.

The health and medical assistance program consisted of dispatching health and medical experts and supplying medical equipment to

TABLE 8.3

Japanese Technical Assistance Experts, by Field

Field	1955	1960	1965	1970
Agriculture	12	42	36	32
Fisheries	2	11	7	31
Construction	8	4	14	28
Heavy industry	0	2	2	8
Mining	0	6	15	16
Light industry	6	11	12	17
Chemical industry	0	3	0	4
Public utilities	0	3	7	13
Transportation	0	9	8	38
Telecommunications	0	14	19	38
Health and welfare	0	16	25	108
Atomic power	0	0	0	0
Business management	0	0	3	3
Education	0	7	3	19
Administration	0	1	3	8
Banking	0	0	0	1
Statistics	0	0	0	1
Advertising	0	0	0	0
Others	0	2	0	7
Total	28	131	154	372

Source: Kaigai Gijutsu Kyoryoku Jigyodan, Gijutsu Kyoryoku Nenpo: 1970, pp. 324-26.

recipient countries. Since the program was started in 1966, an increasing number of Japanese experts in health and medical education have been dispatched: 112 in 1967, 161 in 1968, and 165 in 1969. In contrast, only 10 to 20 health and welfare experts were sent abroad each year in the 1950s and 1960s. [7]

The assistance program in science education was also started in 1966 to improve the overall level of education in developing countries by promoting science education. In view of the need to strengthen the basic understanding of science among large segments of the populations of the developing countries, the program put its main emphasis on in-service training of science teachers at secondary schools. While the importance of science education has been duly recognized, the program has not grown as rapidly as the medical program due partly to the need for a greater command of foreign languages among Japanese experts in science education than among those in medicine.

The agricultural assistance program was started in 1967 to consolidate and expand Japan's already ongoing agricultural cooperation activities. Instead of dispatching experts in specific fields in response to individual requests, this new program aimed at meeting a recipient country's requirements for agricultural development in terms of both physical and institutional aspects. Thus survey teams were sent out to ascertain the manner in which comprehensive and integrated approaches to agricultural development could be undertaken.

Overseas Technical Cooperation Centers

As an alternative approach to the training programs undertaken in Japan, technical training centers have also been set up in Asia, Africa, and Latin America to facilitate the transfer of Japanese technical know-how to the various recipient countries. The first training center of this sort was launched in Dacca in 1960, and a total of 32 such centers had been set up with Japanese assistance by the end of the fiscal year 1971. [8]

Japanese involvement in building these overseas centers has been characterized by fair but limited success. Since the centers are located in the recipient countries, Japanese technical know-how is adapted to local conditions more closely than in the case of the training programs in Japan. In the overseas centers the major portion of Japanese inputs has gone to small-scale light industry, agriculture, fisheries, telecommunications, and health and welfare. A large number of trainees and students have attended courses and received experimental training. However, establishment of the overseas centers has turned out to be an endeavor requiring longer periods of time and larger inputs than were originally envisaged.

Japanese assistance in developing the centers usually has consisted of providing both experts and equipment. Experts are sent from Japan to carry out demonstration and research activities at the centers; they also conduct technical training for their counterparts in developing nations and for trainees. The counterparts are often sent to Japan for accelerated training so they may eventually take over the management of the centers.

For the Agricultural Cooperation Center in Dacca, Japan agreed to provide agricultural machinery and other equipment valued at 36.4 million yen, or about $100,000. Six Japanese experts were then sent to the center to conduct refresher courses for local agricultural extension workers. Later a seventh expert was added plus equipment worth $12,000. While the original plan of operations envisaged the conclusion of Japanese assistance by 1963, it was extended for two more years until June 1965. OTCA then reported that the Japanese experts had completed nine training terms, having trained 315 students during the five years.[9] After the take-over of the center by local personnel, Japan agreed to send four experts, under the Colombo Plan, for two years to help launch the center as an agricultural mechanization training center. Upon completion of these experts' terms, two more experts were sent, also under the Colombo Plan, for two years.

In a similar manner Japanese experts and equipment were sent to a total of 19 countries as part of the institution-building efforts of assistance-receiving countries during the period from April 1955 to March 1971. Out of the total number of 293 experts sent by Japan under the overseas training center program, the largest number, 126, were experts in the field of light industry. The second largest number, 78, were experts in the field of agriculture; 37 were experts in postal service; 22 in fisheries; 18 in health and welfare; and 10 in construction. In addition, by far the largest number of countries received technical advice in the light industry field; these countries (and the number of experts provided them) included the Philippines (1), Singapore (14), South Korea (4), Taiwan (10), Afghanistan (11), Ghana (18), Iran (9), Kenya (25), Uganda (11), and Brazil (7). Countries receiving advice in the field of agriculture and fisheries (and number of experts provided) included Ceylon (10), Cambodia (15), India (58), Indonesia (4), and Pakistan (17). Countries obtaining advisory aid in postal services (and number of experts provided) were Pakistan (11), Thailand (11), and Mexico (12).[10]

To realize the transfer of Japanese technical know-how under varying conditions, the composition of Japanese inputs differed according to recipient countries. At a textile training center in Ghana, for example, the main emphasis has been on production of towels and on a basic dyeing process used on material available in Ghana. Extra efforts have been made for training Ghanaian counterparts to acquire adequate skill for the maintenance of textile machinery. In Brazil intensive training has been conducted in sophisticated methods of dyeing and materials testing. Equipment transferred to Brazil was more sophisticated and complex than equipment sent to Ghana.

In like manner telecommunications centers in Iran and Pakistan have required different levels of training techniques and equipment. In Pakistan installations of telecommunications machinery such as the telephone have to take into account the relatively limited understanding of such systems among the public at large. For public pay telephones, for example, large collection boxes have had to be installed to permit less frequent collection. The warning buzz was implemented in long-distance calls between Rawalpindi and Karachi over the passage of a certain time duration. In Iran on the other hand Japanese experts and equipment were tailored to meet the objectives of Iranian research activities in microwave broadcasting, tie-line, and other relatively advanced technology.

Small-scale industry and vocational training centers in the Philippines and Kenya have also aimed at training technicians and craftsmen to utilize factors available in their respective societies. In the Philippines ceramics, bamboo, and wood processing have received priority attention. In Kenya courses were set up in metal work, electric machinery assembling, sewing machine development, carpentry, machinery repair, and leather utilization. Moreover management of the centers and shops required the adoption of a less rigid organizational setup than that which is common in Japan.

In spite of the general success and advantages of the overseas training center approach, the program has met with a number of operational difficulties and disadvantages. First, since establishment of the centers depends on inputs from both assistance-receiving and donor countries, it tends to be delayed due to nondelivery of the inputs by either side. Due to Japan's rigid budgetary system, she cannot make advance commitments and adopt modifications on such budgeting. And it is often not possible for the recipient-governments to find adequate land and start building until Japanese experts have arrived in the country.

The program has also been hurt by the same problem noted earlier: the difficulty in finding competent Japanese technical experts who can teach at the overseas training centers in English or any other languages used locally. While special efforts have been made by both the experts and sponsoring agencies to enable the experts to acquire proficiency in the commonly used foreign languages, speaking and understanding a second language has turned out to be a formidable task for many of the Japanese experts. It should be noted that foreign language instruction at high schools and colleges in Japan has remained archaic; excessive emphasis on grammatical correctness and on the importance of translating into Japanese has led students to spend much of their time learning an English which everyday users of English often have difficulty understanding. Not only that but most of the high school teachers of English in Japan have had no contact with English-speaking people and have rarely heard English spoken on a daily basis. Reflecting upon such a situation, the chairman of the Development Assistance Committee of OECD Edwin Martin, singled out the lack of linguistic ability among Japanese experts as the major factor "holding back the expansion of its [Japan's] international technical cooperation."[11]

NOTES

1. Japan, Ministry of Foreign Affairs, Japan's Foreign Aid (Tokyo: 1967), pp. 7-8.

2. Japan, Economic Planning Agency, Basic Economic and Social Plan: 1973-77 (Tokyo: 1973).

3. Kaigai Gijutsu Kyoryoku Jigyodan, Gijutsu Kyoryoku Nenpo, (1971), p. 59.

4. Edward G. Seidensticker et al., Han-nichi Kanjo (Tokyo: Nisshin Hodo Shuppan Bu, 1973); Tai Kuo Fei, ed., Nippon-Jin Tono Taiwa (Tokyo: Shakai Shisosha, 1971).

5. Kaigai Gijutsu Jigyodan pp. 72, 94; Kaigai Konsarutingu Kyokai, Arudantai no Kiroku (Tokyo: Engineering Consulting Firms of Japan, 1974), pp. 7-9.

6. Chie Nakane, Tekiyo no Jyoken (Tokyo: Kodansha, 1972); see also Kinichiro Toba, Futatsu no Kao no Nippon-jin (Tokyo: Chuo Koron Sha, 1973).

7. Kaigai Gijutsu Jigyodan, Gijutsu Kyoryoko Nenpo: 1971, pp. 324-25.

8. Much of this section is drawn from Chapter 4 of "Kaigai Gijutsu Kyoryoku Centa Jigyo," Gijutsu Kyoryoku Nenpo: 1971, Kaigai Gijutsu Kyoryoku Jigyo Dan. pp. 113-137.

9. Kaigai Gijutsu Jigyodan, Gijutsu Kyoryoku Nenpo: 1971, p. 119.

10. Ibid., p. 345, Table III, (1)-2.

11. OECD, Development Cooperation: 1972 Review, (1972), p. 174.

9

FORMULATION AND
ADMINISTRATION OF
JAPANESE AID PROGRAM

The formulation and administration of the Japanese aid program are carried out, as noted previously, to protect Japan's kokueki (national interest) and to ultimately attain her national goals. For this purpose not only the Japanese government agencies but also private entities have been involved in the formulation of aid proposals and implementation of aid projects. Among the government agencies closely involved in aid policy formulation and implementation, the most generally influential ones are the Ministry of International Trade and Industry (Tsusansho), the Ministry of Foreign Affairs (Gaimusho), and the Ministry of Finance (Okurasho). At the same time certain prominent members of zaikai, or the business world, also carry a significant amount of weight during the preparatory stages of aid policy formulation and implementation.

FORMULATION OF AID POLICIES

Gaimusho, Tsusansho, and Okurasho are each inclined to serve its own ideas, interests, and constituents in the determination of specific aid policies and projects. As Gaimusho staff members represent Japan at UNCTAD, OECD, and other international forums, they have been rather sensitive to foreign criticism and desirous of quantitative expansion and qualitative improvement of the Japanese aid program. Tsusansho on the other hand has considered itself responsible for the successful implementation and realization of Japan's postwar economic prosperity. It claims it has advocated economic cooperation when, and to the particular extent, it has benefited Japan directly. When Japanese foreign aid was still being considered in terms of the baisho and export incentive measures, Tsusansho took various initiatives in publishing a white paper on economic

cooperation and laying guidelines for firms wishing to take advantage
of funds made available under the aid program. Later Tsusansho set
forth the kaihatsu yunyu scheme examined in Chapter 5. Because of
its influence and power generated through the use of "administrative
guidance," redirection of Japan's basic national policy was to become
possible only after the leaders of Tsusansho became convinced of such
a need for reduction and undertook its own reorganization in 1972. [1]
Meanwhile Okurasho has maintained cautious fiscal and monetary
policies, placing first priority on stable expansion of the national
economy; thus the amounts of increase in grants and contributions to
multilateral aid agencies have often been reduced to give priority to
other proposals related mostly to domestic improvement.

Differing proposals and observations on specific aid issues in
Japan are brought up for reconciliation to the ad hoc Ministerial
Meeting on Overseas Economic Cooperation, designed to coordinate
aid policies among such ministries and agencies as: Tsusansho,
Okurasho, Gaimusho, the Economic Planning Agency, and the Ministry
of Agriculture and Forestry. These ministries and agencies in turn are
supposed to maintain close contact with the three major aid implementing institutions: the Overseas Economic Cooperation Fund (OECF),
the Export-Import Bank of Japan, and the Overseas Technical Cooperation Agency (OTCA). These institutions, however, are placed under the
supervision of different ministries in terms of financing and appointment of officials. OECF is under the supervision of the Economic
Planning Agency, the Export-Import Bank of Japan is under Okurasho,
and OTCA is under Gaimusho. Given such arrangements, it has often
been difficult to reconcile conflicting viewpoints and come up with
uniform aid policies.

Thus in an effort to bring about more systematic formulation of
aid policies, the Japanese government set up the advisory Council
on Overseas Economic Cooperation in 1969. The council then submitted its recommendations for systematic aid formulation in September
1971, pointing out the need to advance uniform economic cooperation
policies that take into consideration both the linkages between technical assistance and capital aid and between official government and
private aid activities. Concerning technical assistance activities,
the council recommended the expansion of programs for human resources
development, particularly in the fields of education and medicine. To
improve efficiency in implementation, it called for the improvement of
administrative arrangements in technical assistance. Overall recommendations called for systematic expansion of Japanese official
development assistance, expansion of the geographic coverage of
development assistance, strengthening of cooperation with international agencies, and improvements in the administrative setup for
implementing aid programs. [2]

In December 1973 the Tanaka government proposed a plan to
systematize Japan's approach toward overseas economic cooperation.

The government's plan envisaged the appointment of a cabinet minister who would supervise economic cooperation activities and the establishment of an agency to be called the Overseas Economic Cooperation Agency. The new minister was to have his own small secretariat assisting him in coordinating Japan's aid policy and in attending various international conferences. On the other hand the new agency would, according to the proposal, absorb not only the existing OTCA (then under the supervision of Gaimusho), but as well an Overseas Trade and Development Cooperation Agency proposed by Tsusansho, and an Overseas Agriculture and Forestry Development agency proposed by the Ministry of Agriculture and Forestry.[3]

Without any direct support of electoral and interest groups within Japan, the reorganization scheme faced strong resistance from sectoral ministries and only part of the original scheme was realized. The new implementing agency was finally set up in August 1974 with the title of Kokusai Kyroyoku Jigyodan (Japan International Cooperation Agency). But its functions consisted mainly of those undertaken by OTCA and Overseas Emigration Agency. While Japan Overseas Cooperation Volunteers were also placed in the jigyodan along some of technical cooperation works related to health, agriculture, forestry, and mining, neither the OECF nor the Export-Import Bank of Japan was touched by the reorganization.[4] As Gaimusho insisted that the issue of economic cooperation was part of foreign policy matters, the Ministry exerted strong pressure against establishment of a post for a strong, independent economic cooperation minister. During the course of defining the jurisdiction of the new minister, his main role was gradually reduced to that of coordinating and explaining about Japan's foreign aid policies at international conferences. No permanent bureaucracy was to be set up to assist him in actual formulation and implementation of the aid policies. Even six months after the post of economic cooperation minister was proposed in the beginning of 1974, it was not formally approved by the Diet.

Whatever may happen as a result of the appointment of the new minister, it is expected that any major changes in Japanese aid policies will follow changes that first take place in Japan's national goals. Such changes are possible only after interaction not only among government agencies but among business, labor, and academic circles. This was the case in the affirmation of vigorous aid measures that emerged in the early 1970s and in officially incorporating into Japan's new national goals, adopted in February 1973, the new economic and social development plan for 1973-77.[5]

The plan itself had earlier been drafted by the Economic Council chaired by Kazutaka Kikawada, president of Tokyo Electric Power Company, in response to a written request made directly by Prime Minister Tanaka regarding ways "to seek the fulfillment of national welfare and the promotion of international collaboration." The 30-member economic council, representing an amalgamation of leaders

TABLE 9.1

Members of Economic Council in 1973

Hideo Aoyama	Professor, Kyoto University
Koichiro Asakai	Adviser, Ministry of Foreign Affairs
Seizi Amaike	Chairman, All Japan Labor Union Conference
Makoto Ichikawa	President, General Council of Trade Unions of Japan
Syuzo Inaba	Chairman, Economic Research Association
Hiroki Imazato	President, Nippon Seiko Co., Ltd.
Yoshizane Iwasa	President, the Fuji Bank, Ltd.
Koshichi Ueno	Vice President, Kansai Electric Power Co., Ltd.
Hideo Edo	President, Mitsui Real Estate Dev. Co., Ltd.
Jiro Enjoji	President, The Nihon Keizai Shimbun (Japan Economic Press)
Hideko Chama	President, Better Living Information Center
Takekazu Ogura	Chairman, Institute of Developing Economies
Kunio Odaka	Emeritus Professor, Tokyo University
Kazutaka Kikawada	President, Tokyo Electric Power Co., Ltd.
Kazuyuki Knono	President, The Taiyo Bank, Ltd.
Michikazu Kono	Vice-President, Bank of Japan
Minoru Segawa	Chairman, The Nomura Securities Co., Ltd.
Eika Takayama	Emeritus Professor, Tokyo University
Hajime Takagi	President, The Shoko Chukin Bank
Motoo Tsuchikawa	Chairman, Nagoya Rail Road Co., Ltd.
Seiichi Tohata	Emeritus Professor, Tokyo University
Toshio Doko	President, Tokyo Shibaura Electric Co., Ltd.
Shigeo Nagano	Chairman, Nippon Steel Corporation
Sohei Nakayama	Counselor, The Industrial Bank of Japan, Ltd
Ichiro Nakayama	Emeritus Professor, Hototsubashi University
Norishige Hasegawa	President, Sumitomo Chemical Co., Ltd.
Kiichiro Hirata	Governor, The Corporation for the Reallocation of Industry and the Development of Coal Mining Areas
Shigeo Horie	President, Institute for International Studies and Training
Teizo Horikoshi	Vice President, Federation of Economic Organization
Tatsuzo Mizukami	Senior Adviser to Board, Mitsui Bussan Co., Ltd.

Source: Economic Planning Agency, Basic Economic and Social Plan: 1973-79 (Tokyo: Ministry of Planning Printing Bureau, 1973) p. 179.

of various groups, consists of 14 businessmen, 5 professors, 4 researchers, 3 representatives of public institutions, 2 labor and trade union officials, 1 publisher, and 1 advisor to a government ministry (see Table 9.1). The council is advised by "specialized members" of the government on specific economic policies and issues through the providing of reference data and materials.

Concerning the issue of overseas economic cooperation, the council recommended that, as part of Japanese national policy, the government raise Japan's overseas financial flow level—currently 1 percent of her GNP—by fiscal 1975; meet the international target of 0.7 percent of GNP for official development assistance as early as possible; make qualitative improvements in the terms and conditions of development assistance; untie all bilateral official loans; expand multilateral assistance; increase massive technical cooperation; and promote economic cooperation on the basis of a long-term perspective.

Neither the basic aid policy formulation process nor the positive measures recommended by the council were expected to change little even after the establishment of the cabinet minister's post for overseas economic cooperation proposed by the Tanaka government in December 1973.

ADMINISTRATION OF AID PROGRAM

Japanese administrative structures and procedures in regard to aid are also designed to protect Japan's kokueki and to fulfill her changing national goals. Japanese government agencies and business firms have maintained an intricate network of consultations through both formal and informal arrangements. Due to Japan's emphasis in aid policy on stabilization of her ties with aid-receiving governments, her aid agencies have tended to neglect the welfare of citizens of the recipient countries.

During the early years of the Japanese aid program, in the 1950s, institutional and procedural arrangements in the program were set up to protect the Japanese economy from any adverse effects. Reparations payments were administered in accordance with strict rules and procedures so as not to threaten the often precarious balance-of-payments position. During the subsequent years of Japanese economic expansion the Japanese government established a number of institutions and agencies designed to implement capital lending, technical assistance, and research programs in a manner that would be protective of Japan's national interests. Among these aid agencies and institutions, the Export-Import Bank of Japan and the OECF, as indicated previously, have emerged as the major institutions for capital lending; moreover, in the field of technical assistance, the OTCA became the dominant government agency designed to provide technical training and advice to developing countries.

When the Japanese government entered into negotiations with various countries for reparations payments, it took administrative steps to ensure that these payments would not adversely affect Japan's balance of payments and hinder her own economic rehabilitation and growth. To control the disbursement of reparations funds, the government established a number of committees and commissions that were to be used for the purpose of screening out reparations projects unfavorable to Japan's interests.

As part of the reparations agreements, Japan and the recipient countries set up bilateral consultative committees to discuss and decide on the implementation of specific reparations projects. The Japanese government then created a reparations division within Gaimusho. The division's director, who was to represent Japan at bilateral consultative committee sessions also attended by representatives of the recipient governments, was to be normally stationed in Tokyo with diplomatic privileges. In addition, within the Japanese bureaucracy appropriate sections of 11 ministries and agencies were designated to handle reparations matters related to their particular ministries and agencies, and their vice-ministers participated in a policy formulation committee chaired by the foreign minister. The aforementioned bilateral consultative commissions involving Japan and the reparations-receiving countries, as well as the coordinating committee among Japanese ministries and agencies, soon became devices for the Japanese government to keep reparations payments under its own control. The reparations payments procedure for the Philippines, outlined below, shows in detail how Japan made sure her own kokueki was protected. [6]

In the Philippines the final users of Japanese goods and services were mostly private firms. In the case of both Burma and Indonesia, these firms were replaced by public corporations and government agencies. On the Japanese side the process was more or less the same for reparations transactions as that used for the Philippines.

As shown in Figure 2, the final user of Japanese goods and services applied to the reparations committee in the Philippines for procurement of particular goods and services from Japan under terms of the reparations agreement between the two countries. The reparations committee then submitted the list of requests to the president of the Philippines with appropriate recommendations from the National Economic Council of the Philippines. Upon receipt of presidential approval, the committee forwarded the list to Tokyo. As the next step, the Philippine reparations commission in Tokyo then proposed an implementation plan, including the list of selected requests, to the Japanese government. At this stage the reparations division of Gaimusho consulted other Japanese ministries concerned to make sure that the proposal would not be against Japan's national interests; only when the proposal was considered within these interests could the Philippine reparation committee announce the implementation plan in the Philippines and issue procurement orders.

136

FIGURE 2

Administration of Japanese Reparations Contract

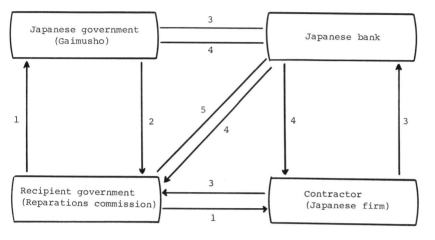

Source: Gaimusho, Keizai Kyoryoku Kyoku, Tenki ni Tatsu Nippi
Keizai Kyoryoku (November 1972), p. 44.

The first institution to become a major instrument of Japanese
capital lending to less-developed countries was the Export-Import
Bank of Japan. The bank has in fact acted almost too effectively as
an instrument of the Japanese government for protecting Japan's
kokueki. While the bank has continually extended credits and loans
to North America, Europe, and Oceania in addition to Asia, Africa,
and Latin America, it had become the main lender of Japanese capital
by the end of the 1950s to less-developed countries as it allocated
a major portion of its lending to them. Funded entirely by the Japanese
government, the bank initially followed closely the conservative
lending policies of the government. While lending terms were kept
stringent, showing little differences from ordinary banking operations
in the early years, later the terms were gradually eased in response
to the government's decision to do so as a result of pressures exerted
by OECD, UNCTAD, and other international institutions (as mentioned
in Chapters 2 and 3). In addition, while easing loan terms, the bank
kept close ties with business firms operating in developing countries.

The bank's predecessor, the Export Bank, had been established
in December 1950 to facilitate exports of heavy machinery. The

Export Bank was then designated as the Export-Import Bank of Japan, in April 1952, to cover not only export but import activities. Following this responsibilities of the bank were further expanded gradually to include financing of overseas investments in 1953 and extending of yen loans directly to foreign governments and corporations in 1958. By the beginning of the 1970s the overall objective of the Bank was substantially broadened

> to facilitate through financial aid Japan's economic interchange mainly in the field of trade, with foreign countries, especially to expand economic cooperation with developing countries, by supplementing or encouraging ordinary financial institutions in their financing of exports, imports and overseas investments, as well as by extending Yen loans to foreign governments and corporations. [7]

The first yen credit extended to India in February 1958 marked the turning point in the bank's operations; the bank then became the main lender of Japanese capital. Export credits such as those given to India were provided to Japanese exporters to enable them to extend suppliers' credits for export of capital goods and technical services. Import credits have since been extended to enable Japanese importers to cover payments for imports of materials that are considered essential for the Japanese economy.

The bank has also provided overseas investment credits to Japanese overseas investors for their enterprises abroad or for their capital participation in joint ventures. Development project credits are provided either to Japanese firms for loans to foreign governments or to foreign governments themselves for development purposes. Such development credits are extended on the condition that they bring about the export of equipment from Japan so as to promote the import of strategic materials to Japan. [8] In this way the bank is in effect implementing the kaihatsu yunyu scheme (described in Chapter 6).

The decisions to extend various loans and credits are based on benefits that Japan may receive from such extension loans and credits. Because of their excessive concern over the impact of foreign credits and loans on the Japanese economy, the managers of the bank have tended to give secondary importance to the impact of credits and loans on the welfare of the people in recipient countries; they have been unduly conscious of the actual amount of lending, as if quantity were the only key factor in development assistance. As its cumulative credit commitments reached $8,730 million by March 1971, the bank was proud to announce that "it has contributed to the development of the economy of Japan and to the promotion of economic cooperation with developing nations."[9]

Reflecting Japan's conservative policy, the terms of yen lending extended by the bank remained stringent for less-developed countries

TABLE 9.2

Terms of Loans Extended to India by Export-Import Bank of Japan

Fiscal Year	Maturity Years	Grace Years	Interest Rate (%)
1957	10	3	5.75, 6.00 and 6.25
1961	15	5	6.00
1963	15	5	6.00
1963	15	5	5.75
1964	15 and 18	5	5.75
1965	15 and 18	5	5.75
1966	15	5	5.75
1967	18	5	5.50
1968	18	5	5.25
1970	18	5	5.25
1971	20	7	5.00
1972	20	7	4.75

Source: Kaigai Keizai Kyoryoku Kikin Shosa Bu (ed.), Kaigai Keizai Kyoryoku Bekkan: 1972, pp. 420-27.

until the early 1970s. In the 1950s and 1960s development loans were extended at the average annual rate of 5.25-6.50 percent for the period of 15-18 years including a grace period of 3-5 years, as shown in Table 9.2.

While controlled by the Government with respect to funds and officer appointments, the bank has kept close ties with the Japanese business establishment. The bank in fact has extended its loans mostly to Japanese firms; as its loans have to be financed partly from private sources, the bank tends to select well-established firms for extending loans. Loans to less-developed countries have been viewed with skepticism by private sources that have provided additional funds needed for the bank's lending activities. The bank is empowered to provide up to 80 percent of the funds required for export credits and up to 50 percent of the funds required for approved overseas investments; the balance has to come from private sources.

The terms and conditions of lending offered by the Export-Import Bank of Japan became a source of foreign criticism by the beginning of the 1960s as the Development Assistance Group was formed and a worldwide development decade was declared by the United Nations General Assembly. In the 1950s Japan justified its strict lending terms by its own low level of per capita income and relatively weak financial position. As the Japanese economy began to expand rapidly, however, it became increasingly difficult to claim any sort of effective aid performance while resorting to the hard-term lending of the bank alone. To meet the increasing demand of less-developed countries for loans and credits with easier terms, the Ikeda government set up OECF in March 1961 as proof of its serious concern for the welfare of aid-receiving countries.

OECF represented an improvement in Japanese aid activities but continued to demonstrate the inadequate aspects of Japanese policy toward economic cooperation. The volume of funds channeled through OECF has been limited in the light of the requirements of less-developed countries and the overall capacity of Japan to provide funds. Japanese firms continued to receive funds directly from OECF for the implementation of various development projects for which loans have been designed, until fiscal year 1972 when the fund made its first "untied loan" to Burma.

The interest rate of loans extended by OECF to foreign governments has ranged from 3-to-4.5 percent with a period of repayment of about 20 years or more. The terms are more concessional tnan those of the Export-Import Bank of Japan. The amount of OECF lending has, however, remained smaller than that of the Export-Import Bank of Japan due to OECF's relatively limited capital availability.

As of March 1971, the total cumulative amount of loans and investment committed by OECF reached $606.1 million, but it was less than half of the $1,488 million of credit commitments made by the Export-Import Bank of Japan in fiscal year 1970 alone. OECF's lending did increase during the following years; but the amount of loans it extended in fiscal year 1972 was approximately $460 million in comparison with $1,890 million committed by the Export-Import Bank of Japan in the same year. [10] The main constraining factor for OECF still has been the small amount of funds provided by the government for projects designed purely for development purposes.

During the first five years after its establishment OECF used its own capital as its basis for lending; this capital was made available from the government's general account budget. Initially the capital consisted of some $15 million derived from the Southeast Asia Development Cooperation Fund, wnich had been established earlier to provide financial resources for subscription to international organizations active in the regional development of Southeast Asia. In subsequent years the government provided additional funds for enlargement of OECF's capital which totaled $491.2 million as of March 1973. However, the additional contributions from the government remained insufficient for the need to finance the increasing number of loan requests. The statute of OECF was amended in 1965 to enable it to borrow from various public sources such as postal savings and post office insurance. At the end of March 1973 the outstanding amount of funds borrowed in this manner by OECF stood at $390.5 million. [11]

During its first few operating years, from 1961 to 1964, OECF extended loans only to Japanese firms engaged in already developed projects. It was not until 1965 that OECF signed a loan agreement with a foreign government. As of the end of March 1973, the amount of OECF loans committed to foreign governments totaled 345 billion yen or about $1,040 million. This total is broken down in the following list of the various nations receiving OECF loans, along with the amounts received, as of March 1973 (as reported by OECF):[12]

Recipients	Amount
Indonesia	158.9
South Korea	93.2
Philippines	29.7
Burma	15.4
Taiwan	12.5
Thailand	10.2
Turkey	8.0
South Vietnam	5.2
Malaysia	4.0
Peru	5.4
Others	2.4
Total	344.9

Since its establishment in 1962, the management and operations of OTCA have been characterized by three features. First, the structure of this agency has been expanded by the addition of new bureaus, departments, offices, and centers that have paralleled OTCA's expanded volume and scope of activities during the mid- and late 1960s. Second, as a government agency, OTCA has accepted for consideration only those aid proposals received by the Japanese government through diplomatic channels. Third, OTCA trainees have had little contact with the Japanese people; by contrast, training centers established overseas tend to be successful and fruitful.

As technical assistance provided by OTCA grew, its institutional structure was also expanded to implement new programs. Initially OTCA merely handled arrangements for receiving foreign trainees and assigning Japanese experts to recipient countries; OTCA received middle- and higher-level trainees and provided them either with group or individual training. For group training OTCA has set up standard courses of study to satisfy the basic requirements of most of the trainees. For individual training OTCA selects government agencies, public institutions, or private firms to provide the training needed for specific requirements. Many of the trainees, particularly in group training, are accommodated at five international training centers (as mentioned in Chapter 8), managed by OTCA for different training purposes.

In 1965, when the Japan Overseas Cooperation Volunteers was formed, the Japanese government entrusted the agency with the responsibility of recruiting and sending out Japanese youths. In the following year, 1966, the Agency added two programs called medical cooperation, and science education cooperation programs. In 1967, two additional departments were established to implement the agricultural development cooperation scheme and the primary products developing cooperation scheme.

As the Japanese technical assistance program grew over the years, OTCA established its representative offices in Bangkok, Dacca, Djakarta, Nairobi, New Delhi, Manila, Phnom Penh, Saigon, Singapore, and Teheran. The Resident Representative of JOCV have also been stationed in Malaysia, Tanzania, Laos, Philippines, Morocco, Kenya, India, Zambia and Malaysia.

In spite of the variety of the Japanese technical assistance program, the representatives dealt with their counterparts who were found only in liaison offices attached to the foreign ministries and other government agencies of the recipient countries. People in the recipient countries had no means of obtaining Japanese technical assistance directly. This approach helped strengthen the position of ruling governments in the recipient countries. The first beneficiaries tended to be officials who occupied strategic posts in the local governments. They were the first ones to make inspection trips and guided tours in Japan. The benefits accruing from their return to their countries have not always been maximized. Since there was virtually no possibility for ordinary people to apply for fellowships and training without support of the recipient governments, they tended to view Japanese technical assistance as either alien to their area or associated with the governments in power.

In summary, Japanese foreign aid policies and programs have been formulated and implemented to enhance Japan's kokueki and to help attain her changing national goals. The formulation and implementation of Japanese aid are characterized by close working relationships between government agencies, business establishments, and academic circles. Among the Government ministries, Gaimusho, Tsusansho, and Okurasho have played influential roles in determination of specific aid policies and measures. Aid policies and measures have not always been coordinated due to conflicting views and interests of the government ministries and agencies. To reconcile conflicting aid policies, the Japanese government has established first an advisory Council on Economic Cooperation and an ad hoc Ministerial Meeting on Economic Cooperation. As a further step to coordinate systematically aid policy formulation and implementation, the Tanaka government proposed in 1974 establishment of a Cabinet Minister in charge of overseas economic cooperation and formation of a Japanese International Cooperation Agency.

Major institutions administering Japanese aid until 1973 were the Overseas Economic Cooperation Fund (OECF), Export-Import Bank of Japan, and Overseas Technical Cooperation Agency (OTCA). Their policies and administrative structures were designed to protect Japan's immediate national interests. They relied exclusively on governmental ries between Japan and recipient countries. The two major lending institutions, the bank and OECF, have expanded substantially their capital and borrowing for lending purposes. OTCA has also expanded its technical assistance activities and established overseas offices. Its institution building program turned out to be most successful. The Japanese people's inability to use English and other internationally spoken languages and their difficulties in adjusting to people of different societies and cultures have made successful implementation of some Japanese technical assistance programs difficult.

NOTES

1. Taro Nawa, Tsusansho (Tokyo: Kyoikusha, 1974), pp. 54-63, and U.S. Department of Commerce, Japan: the Government-Business Relationship (Washington D.C.: Government Printing Office, 1972).

2. Tsusansho, Keizai Kyoryoku no Genjo to Mondai-ten: 1971, pp. 110-111.

3. Asahi Shinbun, December 27, 28, and 29, 1973.

4. Kaihatsu Janaru, vol. 8, no. 14, (August 25, 1974), pp. 16-21.

5. Japan, Economic Planning Agency, Basic Economic and Social Plan: 1973-1977 (Tokyo: Ministry of Finance Printing Bureau, 1973).

6. Baisho Mondai-kai, Nippon no Baisho (Tokyo: 1963) p. 88. The ministries and agencies are the Economic Planning Agency, Ministry of Finance (Okurasho), Ministry of Education (Monbusho), Ministry of Health and Welfare (Koseisho), Ministry of Agriculture (Norinsho), Ministry of International Trade and Industry (Tsusansho), Ministry of Transportation (Unyusho), Ministry of Postal Communication (Yuseisho), Ministry of Construction (Kensetsusho), and Ministry of Labor (Rodosho).

7. The Export-Import Bank of Japan, Annual Report: April 1970-March 31, 1971, p. 1.

8. The Export-Import Bank of Japan: Its Role and Function (June 1971), published by the bank, pp. 12-13.

9. Ibid., p. 12.

10. Overseas Economic Cooperation Fund, Annual Report, April 1, 1972-March 31, 1973 (Tokyo: 1973) pp. 5-17; and Export-Import Bank of Japan, Annual Report: April 1972-March 1973 (Tokyo: 1973) pp. 8-19. The exchange rate is 360 yen to one dollar until fiscal year 1970, 336.4 yen to one dollar in fiscal year 1971, 308 yen to one dollar from April 1972 to January 1973 and 270 yen to one dollar for February and March 1973.

11. Overseas Economic Cooperation Fund, OECF: Its Role and Activities (Tokyo: 1973) pp. 4-10.

12. Overseas Economic Cooperation Fund, Annual Report (April 1, 1972-March 31, 1973) p. 10.

For the 20-year period from 1953 to 1973 Japanese foreign aid was extended for the purpose of protecting Japan's kokueki (national intere and ultimately attaining two basic national goals: her own national development and international ascendancy. Five immediate objectives of Japanese aid were (1) to spur the reconstruction and economic grow of Japan, (2) to establish diplomatic ties with neighboring countries, (3) to maintain a political, economic, and social system beneficial to Japan, (4) to raise Japanese per capita income, and (5) to assert Japan's leadership position in the Asian region and to attain her prope place in the global community. As the nature of Japan's basic nationa goals changed over the years, so did her priorities given to various aid objectives. Until the middle 1960s, Japanese aid was formulated and implemented for immediate commercial objectives and domestic prosperity; since then aid became increasingly directed to the improve ment of the societal welfare of Japan as a whole and to the pursuit of her proper role in the regional and global communities.

The Japanese government has claimed that Japan has been providi aid to less-developed countries mainly because international peace ar a viable world economy, essential for Japan's own security and pros- perity, depend on improvements in the standard of living in the less- developed countries. The Japanese leaders have also asserted that foreign aid has been a responsibility of Japan, as a member of kokusa shakai (the international community), toward the less fortunate coun- tries of the world. Furthermore they have claimed that the volume of Japanese aid has been increased substantially and the terms of her aid improved noticeably in spite of both a limited amount of available resources and numerous domestic problems existing in Japan. In response to recommendations from such international groups as the U. N. Conference on Trade and Development (UNCTAD) and the Organi zation for Economic Cooperation and Development (OECD), the govern ment of Japan has pledged that Japan would, as soon as she can, allocate at least 0.7 percent of her gross national product (GNP) for official development assistance (ODA).

The overall volume of so-called aid, officially known as the total financial flow from Japan to less-developed countries and multilateral institutions, indeed increased gradually until the middle of the 1960s and rapidly after that. This increase in the overall financial flow, however, resulted more from a rapid expansion of private capital and "other official" flows than from an increase in official development assistance flows, which alone should properly be considered as genuine Japanese aid resources.

The total financial flow increased from $380 million in 1960 to $490 million in 1965, to $1,800 million in 1970, and to more than $5,800 million in 1973. As a result the total financial flow, as a percentage of Japan's GNP, increased from a little more than one-half of 1 percent in the early 1960s to nearly 1.0 percent by the beginning of the 1970s. In 1973 the share of GNP represented by aid flow climbed to 1.42 percent, fulfilling a pledge made by Japan, that she would allocate at lease 1 percent of her GNP for overall aid. Moreover Japan's official development assistance expanded substantially after 1960, though it has never reached the level promised for it by the government; it amounted to $105 million in 1960 but to $458 million ten years later in 1970. Within the next three years, the amount more than doubled and passed the $1 billion level in 1973. In spite of this substantial increase in Japan's ODA, its share of Japan's GNP has changed relatively little due to the equally high rate of growth in Japan's GNP, which continued until 1973. The ODA share has averaged about 0.25 percent, or about 0.10 percent below the average annual rate for Development Assistance Committee (DAC) countries as a whole. In the field of technical assistance, Japan's contribution has remained marginal despite the feeling on the part of the Japanese government that Japanese technical know-how is ideally suited for application in less-developed countries. The scale of Japanese technical aid expanded noticeably but continued to be smaller than the comparable contributions of such other major donors as France, Germany, the United Kingdom, and the United States. The extent of Japan's multilateral contribution, on the other hand, was relatively small in the beginning (early 1960s) but began increasing substantially in the middle of the 1960s. The total value of multilateral Japanese ODA was $10 million in the early 1960s, then jumped to $18 million in 1965, to $87 million in 1970, and to $246 million in 1973. Consequently the share of multilateral ODA in total Japanese ODA doubled from 10.1 percent in 1967 to 21.8 percent in 1972.

Japan's "other official" flows (OOF) and private capital flows have expanded more than ODA flows and continued to be the largest components of Japanese aid. Japan has maintained its status as the largest supplier of OOF since the middle of the 1960s; in 1970, she supplied $694 million in OOF, while the second largest supplier, the

United States, extended only $168 million in OOF. Two years later Japan's OOF increased to $856 million, and in 1973 it increased to $1,179 million, while the OOF of the United States, and the other major donor countries, remained more or less the same. The increase in the flows of private resources has been more substantial than any other components of the total financial flow from Japan to less-developed countries and multilateral institutions. The amount of private flows jumped from $103 million in 1960 to $620 million in 1970 and then doubled almost every two years, totaling $3,650 million in 1973.

Initially Japanese aid took the form of baisho, or reparations payments. Its primary objective was political—the recovery of Japanese sovereignty over her territories held by the Allied powers since World War II and the establishment of diplomatic relations with neighboring countries of East and Southeast Asia. Once the basic decision had been made to pay the baisho, Japan endeavored to protect, and enhance her kokueki through the implementation of both reparations and reparation-like payments (economic cooperation grants). Japan agreed to pay reparations and reparation-like payments to Burma, the Khmer Republic (Cambodia), Indonesia, Laos, Malaysia, Singapore, South Vietnam, South Korea, Thailand, and the Philippines. Until 1972 such Communist countries as Mainland China, North Korea, and North Vietnam were excluded from the list of countries with which Japan made efforts to set up diplomatic relations and make reparations payments. However, when the People's Republic of China and the Democratic Republic of Vietnam normalized their diplomatic relations with Japan, respectively in 1972 and 1973, they demanded no reparations from Japan.

The reparations and reparation-like payments which Japan agreed to pay amounted to about $1.5 billion: $1 billion in reparations and $0.5 billion in reparation-like payments. The payments amounted to less than one-fifth of 1 percent of Japan's GNP and no more than a few percent of Japan's national budget. Thus the baisho caused relatively little burden on the Japanese economy. Rather, the payments have seemed to contribute to the current Japanese aid objective—the continuing recovery and consolidation of the Japanese economy through the opening up and development of new markets for Japanese goods in Southeast Asia.

According to the economic valuation analysis, the terms of Japanese aid loans eased noticeably, but not as much as those of other donor countries, during the 15-year period from 1958 to 1973. Both face and grant value of Japanese aid loans increased during the same period. The terms of loans were eased to contain a weighted average grant cost-element of 17.5 percent in 1958 to 43.0 percent in 1973. Although various countries of Latin America and Africa began to receive increasing numbers and amounts of Japanese aid loans in the early 1970s, more than three-fourths of total cumulative Japanese loans extended during the entire period went to Asia. Within Asia, loan preference earlier accorded to the Far Eastern and South Asian countries was gradually shifted to Southeast Asian countries after the middle of the 1960s. The basic decision whether or not to extend an official aid loan has been based on political considerations, as shown in the case of both South Korea and Taiwan. Once a decision is made to extend loans to developing countries, Japan has usually provided softer loans to the relatively less developed among the developing countries, such as Indonesia and Burma, and harder loans to the relatively more developed among them, such as Brazil and Mexico.

Rapid economic growth in Japan in the 1960s, centering around heavy industrialization, created widening trade imbalances in favor of Japan, increased Japan's dependence on overseas supplies of raw materials and primary products, and caused a deterioration in Japan's environmental conditions. To help relieve these problems, the Japanese government set forth as part of its foreign aid program a scheme called kaihatsu yunyu or "development-cum-import". According to this scheme, Japanese capital and technical aid was designed to both develop natural resources and process them in aid-receiving countries for eventual export to Japan or third countries. In the actual implementation of the scheme, however, Japanese capital and technology were directed more to countries with substantial energy and mineral resources than to resource-poor countries. Many of the resource-rich countries had already been enjoying trade imbalances with Japan that were in their favor. During the energy crisis of late 1973 and early 1974, Japan seemed to place the highest priority in the allocation of her aid resources on securing oil, the shortage of which would threaten not only the material prosperity but the actual survival of Japan.

The second major set of national goals of postwar Japan involved ascendancy in the international arena; in this endeavor Japan has been partially successful. After she regained her sovereignty in 1952 she endeavored to secure first her membership, and then a leadership position, in the Asian regional community. In the area of global multilateral aid, Japan has played a comparatively less influential role, although she has become a key member of such multilateral aid institutions as the World Bank and the U. N. Development Programme (UNDP).

During the early 1950s, Japan first entered and consolidated its membership position in ECAFE and the Colombo Plan. She later joined or helped establish regional institutions and programs designed for mainly economic but also political cooperation. Among these cooperative programs, the Mekong Project, the Asian Development Bank and the Ministerial Conference for Economic Development of Southeast Asia emerged as major endeavors actively supported by Japan. In the latter two, Japan eventually became the most important member because of her financial and personnel inputs.

Japan became a legitimate member of the global community when she formally entered the United Nations in 1956 and a member of OECD,

147

an organization known as a "rich men's club" in 1964. But Japanese participation in and her contribution to global institutions and programs have been less active and forthcoming than in regional endeavors. While Japan has established a fairly important membership in such global aid agencies as the World Bank and the UNDP, Japan's financial and personnel inputs remained relatively small and only to the minimal extent required. In short, Japan's involvement in global aid agencies reflected the policy of Otsukiai.

Japan also extended her technical assistance within the framework of government-to-government contacts. The weakest part of Japanese people in international cooperation was revealed hinting that increased Japanese aid would not necessarily bring about friendly and harmonious relations between Japan and recipient countries.

Japanese technical assistance itself expanded its scope in the late 1960s. But it has not been very successful, contrary to the claim made by Japanese official sources that Japan could be most effective in transferring modern technical know-how in suitable form to less-developed countries. The main reasons for the late expansion and limited success seem to be the following. First, Japanese defeat in World War II and subsequent occupation of the country until 1952 closed Japan from contact with other countries including the newly emerging independent nations. By the time Japan regained her sovereignty, British and French had returned to Southeast Asia, followed by the Americans who filled in any remaining vacuum. Southeast Asians, furthermore, were suspicious of any possible return of Japanese as a move toward re-establishment of Japanese hegemony. Secondly, Japan needed its own skilled manpower to make possible both recovery from the devastation of the War and then her economic expansion in the 1960s. As industrialization accelerated in the 1960s, it caused severe labor shortages particularly in the engineering and managerial fields. Third, until the beginning of the 1970s, the Japanese government had paid little serious attention to technical assistance as a desirable form of promoting development of aid-recipient countries. Technical assistance was not an attractive form of aid since it brought about little tangible beneficial return to Japan. Fourth, there have been few Japanese experts who are qualified technically and linguistically to undertake the assignment. Few Japanese experts could explain in English to trainees and counterparts the application of new techniques. Fifth, not so many Japanese sufficiently understood the cultural and social traditions of the host countries and therefore had great difficulty in communicating and establishing sound relationships with the local staff people.

Japanese foreign aid policies and programs have been formulated and implemented to enhance Japan's kokueki and to help attain her changing national goals. The formulation and implementation of Japanese aid has been characterized by close working relationships between governmental agencies, business establishments, and academic circles. Among the Government ministries, Gaimusho, Tsusansho, and Okurasho have played influential roles in determination of specific aid policies and measures. Aid policies and measures have not always been well coordinated due to conflicting views and interests of the government ministries and agencies. To reconcile aid policies, the Japanese government has established an advisory Council on Economic Cooperation and an ad hoc Ministerial Meeting on Economic Coopera- tion. As a further step to coordinate systematically aid policy formula- tion and imolementation, the Tanaka government proposed in 1974 the establishment of a Minister in charge of overseas economic cooperation and the merger of various aid-administering agencies into an inter- national cooperation agency.

During the 20 year period ending in 1973, major institutions administering Japanese aid were the Overseas Economic Cooperation Fund (OECF), Export-Import Bank of Japan, and Overseas Technical Cooperation Agency (OTCA). Their administrative structures were designed to protect Japan's immediate national interest and aid policy measures, for example, gradual easement of the terms of aid loans and credits. They relied exclusively on governmental ties between Japan and recipient countries. The two lending institutions, the Bank and OECF, have expanded substantially their capital and lending resources. OTCA also expanded and established its overseas offices. Its institu- tion building program turned out to be most successful. Japanese people's lack of command of English and other languages internationally spoken and their difficulties in adjusting themselves with people of different societies and cultures made rather difficult the successful implementation of some of Japanese technical assistance programs.

GRANT VALUE AND GRANT ELEMENT OF FOREIGN AID LOANS

The grant value of an aid loan is the difference between the face value of the loan and the present value of interest payments and principal payments, discounted at an appropriate rate of interest.

The present value of aggregate future repayments, P, is the sum of (1) the present value of interest payments during the grace period, P_1, (2) the present value of principal repayments, P_2, and (3) the present value of interest payments made after grace period, P_3.

$$P_1 = \int_0^G iLe^{-qt}\,dt$$

$$= iL \int_0^G e^{-qt}\,dt = iL\,\frac{-1}{q}\,e^{-qt}\Bigg]_0^G$$

$$= \frac{i}{q}\,L\,(1 - e^{-qG})$$

if i = interest rate
           L = face value of the loan
           G = grace period
           q = discount rate

$$P_2 + P_3 = \int_G^T iL\left(1 - \frac{t - G}{T - G}\right)e^{-qt}\,dt + \int_G^T \frac{L}{T - G}\,e^{-qt}\,dt$$

$$= \frac{L}{T - G}\int_G^T e^{-qt}\,dt + iL\int_G^T \frac{T}{T - G}\,e^{-qt} - iL\int_G^T \frac{L}{T - G}\,e^{-qt}\,dt$$

$$= \frac{L}{q(T - G)}\left\{-1\,e^{-qt} - iTe^{-qt} + ie^{-qt}\left(t + \frac{1}{q}\right)\right\}\Bigg]_G^T$$

Source: Compiled by the author from formula developed by Goran Ohlin, Foreign Aid Policies Reconsidered (Paris: OECD, 1966), Annex.

$$= \frac{L}{q(T-G)}\left(-e^{-qt} + \frac{ie^{-qt}}{q}\right)\Bigg|_G^T + \frac{L}{q(T-G)}\left(-iTe^{-qt} + ite^{-qt}\right)\Bigg|_G^T$$

$$= \left(1 - \frac{i}{q}\right)L\frac{e^{-qG} - e^{-qT}}{q(T-G)} + \frac{i}{q}Le^{-qG}$$

$$P = P_1 + P_2 + P_3 = \frac{i}{q}L + \left(1 - \frac{i}{q}\right)\left(\frac{e^{-qG} - e^{-qT}}{q(T-G)}\right)L$$

Therefore, the grant value, GV, is shown as follows.

$$GV = L - P = \left(1 - \frac{i}{q}\right)\left(1 - \frac{e^{-qG} - e^{-qT}}{q(T-G)}\right)L$$

And, the grant element, GE, is as shown below.

$$GE = GV/L = \left(1 - \frac{i}{q}\right)\left(1 - \frac{e^{-qG} - e^{-qT}}{q(T-G)}\right)L$$

Example:

    L = loan amounting to $30.0 million

    i = interest rate of 3 percent

    q = discount rate of 10 percent

    G = grace period of 5 years

    T = maturity period of 15 years

    e = base of natural log of 2.718

Grant element, GE, will be:

$$GE = (1 - 0.03/0.10)\left(1 - \frac{2.718^{-0.10\times5} - 2.718^{-0.10\times15}}{0.10(15-5)}\right)$$

$$= 0.7 \times (1 - 0.6 + 0.223)$$

$$= 0.43162$$

$$= 43.16\%$$

Grant value, GV, will be:

$$GV = GE \times L$$

$$= \$30.0 \text{ million} \times 0.43162$$

$$= \$12.9486 \text{ million}$$

JAPANESE FOREIGN AID LOANS (1958-73)

cal Year		Country	Loan ($ million)	Grant Element	Grant Value
1.	1958	India	50.0	.1752	8.760
	Subtotal		50.0		
2.	1959	Paraguay	3.8	.1808	.687
	Subtotal		3.8		
3.	1960	South Vietnam	7.5	.1985	1.489
	Subtotal		7.5		
4.	1961	India	80.0	.2466	19.728
5.		Pakistan	20.0	.2466	4.932
6.		Brazil	17.5	.2090	3.658
	Subtotal		117.5		
7.	1962	Pakistan	25.0	.2466	6.165
	Subtotal		25.0		
8.	1963	India	15.0	.2466	3.699
9.		Pakistan	30.0	.2620	7.860
0.		India	65.0	.2620	17.030
	Subtotal		110.0		
1.	1964	Pakistan	30.0	.2620	7.860
2.		India	60.0	.2620	15.720
3.		Brazil	7.7	.1645	1.266
4.		Brazil	24.9	.1876	4.671
	Subtotal		122.6		
5.	1965	Taiwan	50.0	.3664	18.320
6.		Taiwan	100.0	.2416	24.160
7.		Korea	200.0	.4693	93.860
8.		India	60.0	.2620	15.720
9.		Iran	17.0	.2619	4.452
0.		Chile	6.2	.1511	.937
1.		Argentina	10.2	.155	1.541
2.		Sri Lanka	5.0	.1600	.800
	Subtotal		448.4		
3.	1966	Pakistan	30.0	.2620	7.860
4.		IDB	10.0	.3083	3.083
5.		Indonesia	30.0	.2126	6.378
6.		Uganda	2.8	.2807	.786
7.		Yugoslavia	5.0	.1600	.800
8.		Tanzania	5.6	.2807	1.572
9.		Kenya	5.6	.2807	1.572
0.		Sri Lanka	5.0	.1600	.800
1.		Brazil	13.3	.1876	2.495
2.		Malaysia	50.0	.3429	17.145

Fiscal Year	Country	Loan ($ million)	Grant Element	Grant Va
33.	Nigeria	30. 0	. 2807	8. 421
34.	India	42. 5	. 2620	11. 135
35.	Mexico	10. 0	. 2274	2. 274
36. 1966	India	2. 5	. 2090	. 523
37.	Pakistan	30. 0	. 2620	7. 860
Subtotal		272. 3		
38. 1967	Indonesia	50. 0	. 3610	18. 050
39.	Indonesia	45. 0	. 2940	13. 230
40.	India	7. 0	. 2620	1. 834
41.	India	6. 1	. 2774	1. 692
42.	India	38. 9	. 2973	11. 564
43.	Sri Lanka	5. 0	. 2355	1. 178
44.	Thailand	30. 0	. 3772	11. 316
45.	Pakistan	30. 0	. 2972	8. 916
46.	Thailand	30. 0	. 2620	7. 860
Subtotal		242. 0		
47. 1968	Indonesia	75. 0	. 5054	37. 905
48.	Indonesia	7. 0	. 2940	2. 058
49.	India	16. 83	. 3069	5. 165
50.	Sri Lanka	5. 0	. 3137	1. 568
51.	IDB	10. 0	. 1990	1. 990
52.	Afghanistan	2. 0	. 4115	. 823
53.	Pakistan	30. 0	. 3137	9. 411
54.	India	28. 17	. 3137	8. 837
55.	Burma	30. 0	. 4458	13. 375
56.	Khmer Republic	4. 2	. 4458	1. 872
57.	Philippines	30. 0	. 3283	9. 849
Subtotal		238. 2		
58. 1969	Mexico	8. 0	. 1650	1. 320
59.	India	19. 56	. 3069	6. 003
60.	Indonesia	75. 0	. 5054	37. 905
61.	Indonesia	6. 6	. 2940	1. 940
62.	Sri Lanka	5. 0	. 3137	1. 568
63.	Colombia	2. 2	. 1418	. 312
64.	CABEI	6. 4	. 2077	1. 329
65.	Mexico	3. 1	. 1481	. 459
66.	Pakistan	30. 0	. 3137	9. 411
67.	India	25. 44	. 3137	7. 981
68.	India	7. 0	. 2973	2. 081
69.	Nepal	1. 0	. 2412	. 241
Subtotal		189. 3		
70. 1970	CABEI	5. 0	. 1459	. 729
71.	Indonesia	100. 0	. 5054	50. 540
72.	Mexico	0. 5	. 1391	. 070

(continued

154

cal Year	Country	Loan (million)	Grant Element	Grant Value
.	India	25.4	.3069	7.795
.	Singapore	8.2	.2972	2.437
.	South Vietnam	4.5	.1868	.841
.	IDB	10.0	.1705	1.705
?.	Sri Lanka	5.0	.3610	1.805
.	Mexico	2.4	.1380	.331
».	Korea	20.0	.1752	3.504
	Subtotal	181.0		
». 1971	India	29.7	.3610	10.721
.	India	18.0	.3257	5.863
:.	Brazil	1.9	.1996	.379
.	Turkey	31.6	.3429	10.835
..	India	24.1	.3069	7.396
..	Indonesia	151.9	.5388	81.843
».	Burma	11.8	.5388	6.358
».	Indonesia	109.5	.4464	48.880
».	Sri Lanka	3.5	.3610	1.263
».	Korea	35.1	.1752	6.149
».	Mexico	2.5	.1447	.362
:.	Taiwan	26.2	.2558	6.702
».	South Vietnam	18.7	.5385	10.075
:.	IDB	23.4	.1611	3.770
:.	Colombia	0.2	.1310	0.026
»..	Mexico	8.9	.1534	1.365
».	Philippines	76.0	.4693	35.666
».	Colombia	0.2	.1310	.028
».	Turkey	10.81	.3772	4.077
».	Mexico	7.4	.1447	1.070
).	Korea	88.4	.4030	35.625
«.	Peru	17.5	.5003	8.755
:.	South Vietnam	6.6	.5388	3.556
:.	Mexico	1.0	.1447	.145
«.	Sri Lanka	11.4	.3791	4.322
:.	India	100.6	.3791	38.137
».	Peru	44.1	.3086	13.609
7.	Peru	12.9	.3086	3.981
:.	Singapore	2.6	.3772	.981
».	Malaysia	58.5	.4459	26.085
).	Malaysia	58.5	.3463	20.258
1.	Burma	15.0	.5388	8.082
	Subtotal	1,008.51		
:. 1972	Thailand	110.4	.4874	53.809
:.	Thailand	26.0	.4874	12.672
«.	Thailand	39.0	.3656	14.258

Fiscal Year	Country	Loan ($ million)	Grant Element	Grant Va
115.	Thailand	32.4	.3656	11.845
116.	Mexico	3.0	.1595	.478
117.	Indonesia	175.5	.5388	94.559
118.	Yugoslavia	30.0	.2558	7.674
119.	Korea	25.0	.4693	11.733
120.	Korea	25.0	.3083	7.708
121.	Mexico	0.8	.1534	.123
122.	Burma	65.4	.5388	35.237
123.	CABEI	2.0	.1790	.358
124.	Nigeria	20.0	.3791	7.582
125.	Ethiopia	12.0	.4332	5.198
126.	Brazil	178.6	.1705	30.451
127.	Philippines	40.0	.4458	17.832
128.	Paraguay	12.7	.4115	5.226
129.	Pakistan	37.7	.1463	5.516
130.	Pakistan	4.3	.3791	1.630
131.	South Vietnam	3.5	.5388	1.886
132.	Chile	2.9	.1468	.426
133.	Chile	8.8	.2774	2.441
134.	Pakistan	26.8	.4233	11.344
135.	Korea	20.0	.3943	8.466
136.	India	38.2	.4856	18.549
137.	India	42.9	.4233	18.159
138.	Zambia	30.0	.3791	11.373
139.	Kenya	11.0	.3773	4.150
140.	Singapore	29.2	.2972	8.678
141.	Burma	10.0	.5388	5.388
142.	Indonesia	74.7	.5388	40.248
	Subtotal	1,137.8		
143. 1973	Egypt	15.6	.1263	1.970
144.	Egypt	10.0	.3971	3.971
145.	Madagascar	13.6	.4332	5.891
146.	Indonesia	9.7	.5868	5.691
147.	Syria	28.8	.4233	12.191
148.	Sri Lanka	11.4	.4233	4.825
149.	Burma	37.7	.5388	20.312
150.	Indonesia	145.1	.6096	88.452
151.	Costa Rica	14.0	.3791	5.307
152.	Mexico	32.5	.1595	5.183
153.	Brazil	23.4	.1595	3.732
154.	Brazil	39.0	.1595	6.220
155.	Brazil	16.2	.1635	2.648
156.	Philippines	34.4	.5195	17.870
157.	Zaire	112.0	.4618	51.721
158.	IDB	16.2	.1652	2.676
	Subtotal	559.6		
	Grand Total	4,713.5		

Note: The Japanese fiscal year begins on April 1 and ends on March 31.
Source: Tsusansho, Keizai Kyoryoku no Genjo to Mondai-ten: 1973 (Tokyo: 1973), pp. 16
79.

SELECTED BIBLIOGRAPHY

PUBLIC DOCUMENTS

In Japanese

Gaimusho (Japan Ministry of Foreign Affairs). Ajiya no Chi-iki
     Kyoryoku Kiko. Tokyo: Nippon Kokusai Mondai Kenkyu Jo, 1971.

_____. Biruma no Jiryoku Kosei Rosen to Wagakuni no Keizai Kyoryoku.
     Tokyo: Okurasho Insatsu Kyoku, 1972.

_____. Gaimusho Chosa Geppo. monthly.

_____. Kokuren Sokai no Jigyo. annual.

_____. Kokuren Keizai Shakai Rijikai no Jigyo. annual.

_____. Nippon no Baisho: Sono Genjo to Mondai-ten. Tokyo: Sekai
     Janaru Sha, 1963.

_____. Sekai Keizai no Kadai: 1972. Tokyo: 1972.

_____. Tai Chuka Minkoku Keizai Kyoryoku Chosa Hokoku Sho. Tokyo:
     1971.

_____. Tenki ni Tatsu Nippi Keizai Kyoryoku. Tokyo: 1973.

_____. Waga Gaiko no Kinkyo. Tokyo. annual.

_____. Zenshin suru kisutan Keizai. Tokyo: 1971.

Gyosei Kanri Cho. Gyosei Kiko Zu: 1972. Tokyo: 1972.

Kagaku Gijutsu Cho Shigen Chosa Jo. Nippon no Shigen Zusetsu.
     Tokyo: 1971.

_____. Sekai no Ten-nen Gasu Shigen. Tokyo: 1971.

Kaigai Gijutsu Kyoryoku Jigyo Dan. Gijutsu Kyoryoku Nenpo. Annual.

_____. OTCA: Gaiyo. Annual.

Kaigai Keizai Kyoryoku Kikin. Kaigai Keizai Kyoryoku Binran. Annual.

Kankyo Cho. Kankyo Hakusho. Annual.

Keiai Kikaku Cho. Keizai Hakusho. Annual.

_____. Keizai Shakai Kihon Keikaku. Tokyo: 1973.

_____. Kokumin Seikatsu Hakusho. Tokyo: annual.

_____. Zusetsu Keizai Hakusho. Annual.

_____. Shin Keizai Shakai Hatten Keikaku: 1970-1975. Tokyo: 1971.

Keizai Shingikai Shigen Kenkyu Iinkai. Kokusaika Jidai no Shigen Mondai. Tokyo: 1970.

Kokumin Seikatsu Shingi Kai. Ningen Kankyo Seibi eno Shishin. Tokyo: 1970.

_____. Shorai no Kokumin Seikatsu Zo: 20-nen go no Bijon. Tokyo: 1966.

Kosei Sho. Kosei Hakusho. Annual.

Naikaku Sori Daijin Kanbo Koho Shitsu. Yoron Shosa Nenkan. Annual.

Sangyo Kozo Shingi Kai. 70-nen dai no Tsusho Sangyo Seisaku. Tokyo: 1971.

_____. Nippon no Taigai Keizai Seisaku. Tokyo: Daiyamondo Sha, 1972.

Sorifu Tokei Kyoku. Nippon Tokei Nenkan. Tokyo: Nippon Tokei Kyokai-Mainichi Shimbun Sha. Annual.

Tsusho Sangyo Sho. Keizai Kyoryoku no Genjo to Mondai-ten. Annual.

_____. Tsusho Hakusho. Annual.

Other Languages

Japanese Government Sources

Councillors Room, Prime Minister's Secretariat. Public Opinion Surveys in Japan: 1959-1960. Tokyo: 1960.

Consulate General of Japan. Japan Report. New York: monthly.

Economic Planning Agency. Economic and Social Development Plan: 1967-71. Tokyo: 1967.

_____. New Economic and Social Development Plan: 1970-1975. Tokyo: 1971.

_____. Basic Economic and Social Plan: 1973-1977. Tokyo: 1973.

Environment Agency. Pollution Related Diseases and Relief Measures in Japan. Tokyo: 1972.

_____. White Paper on Pollution in Japan: 1971. Tokyo: Business Intercommunications, 1971.

_____. Water Pollution Control in Japan. Tokyo: 1972.

_____. Air Pollution Control in Japan. Tokyo: 1972.

Export-Import Bank of Japan. Annual Report. Annual.

_____. Its Role and Function. Tokyo: 1971.

Institute of International Affairs. White Papers of Japan: 1969-1970. Tokyo: Nippon Kokusai Mondai Kenkyu Jo, 1971.

Ministry of Foreign Affairs. Some Features of Japan's Development Assistance. Tokyo: 1961.

_____. Diplomatic Bluebook for 1971. Tokyo: 1972.

_____. Japan's Foreign Aid. Tokyo: 1967.

_____. Japan in the United Nations. Tokyo: 1969.

_____. Japan and Asian Development. Tokyo: 1972.

_____. Development of Environmental Protection in Japan. Tokyo: 1973.

Overseas Economic Cooperation Fund. Annual Report.

_____. Its Role and Activities. Tokyo: 1973.

Permanent Mission of Japan to the United Nations. Japan's Commitment to U. N. University. Press Release. June 18, 1973.

_____. Japan's Contribution to Droughtstricken Saharian Countries in Africa. Press release. June 13, 1973.

Public Sources in Other Languages

Asian Development Bank, Annual Report. Manila.

Committee for the Coordination of Investigations of the Lower Mekong Basin, Annual Report. Bangkok.

International Bank for Reconstruction and Development. World Bank Operations: Sectoral Programs and Policies. Baltimore: Johns Hopkins University Press, 1972.

Organisation for Economic Co-operation and Development. Development Cooperation. Paris: annual.

_____. Investing in Developing Countries. Paris: 1972.

_____. Monetary Policy in Japan. Paris: 1972.

_____. Resources for the Developing World: the Flow of Financial Resources to Less Developed Countries, 1962-1968. Paris: 1970.

United Nations. Official Records of the General Assembly.

_____. Official Records of Economic and Social Council.

_____. External Financing of Economic Development: International Flow of Long-term Capital and Official Donations, 1962-1966. New York: 1968.

_____. Report on Special United Nations Fund for Economic Development. New York: 1953. E/238.

_____. Study of the Capacity of the United Nations Development System. New York: 1969. 2 vols. DP/5.

_____. United Nations Development Programme: Report of the Governing Council. New York: semi-annually.

United Nations Development Programme. Pre-Investment News. New York: monthly.

_____. Action UNDP. New York: bi-monthly.

_____. UNDP Business Bulletin. New York: monthly.

United Nations Department of Economic and Social Affairs. Foreign
Investment in Developing Countries. New York: 1968. E/4446.

____. World Plan of Action for Application of Science and Technology
to Development. New York: 1971. E/4962/Rev. 1.

____. Statistical Yearbook. New York: annual.

United Nations Economic Commission for Asia and the Far East.
Economic Survey of Asia and the Far East. Bangkok: annual.

United Nations Economic Commission for Latin America. Economic
Survey of Latin America: 1970. New York: 1972. E/CN.
12/866/Rev. 1.

United Nations Educational, Scientific, and Cultural Organization.
Science and Technology in Asian Development. Paris: 1970.

United States Department of Commerce. Japan: the Government-Business Relationship. Washington D. C.: 1972.

____. Survey of Current Business. Washington D. C.: monthly.

United States Department of Agriculture. Japanese Overseas Aid and
Investments: Their Potential Effects on World and U. S. Farm
Exports. Washington D. C.: 1972.

United Nations. Multinational Corporation in World Development.
New York: 1973. St/ECA/190.

BOOKS AND ARTICLES

In Japanese

Ajiya Keizai Kenkyu Jo. Ajiya Shokoku no Ekinai Kyoryoku to Enjo.
Tokyo: Ajiya Keizai Kekyu Jo, 1967.

Ajia Seinen Renraku Kaigi and Mushakoji, Kinhide. eds. Futtota
Nippon Jin. Tokyo: Daiyamondo Sha, 1971.

Azuma, Katsuhiko. "Tsuka Kiki kano Ma boku Mondai Senryaku
Jo-Ge," Ekonomisuto, May 1, 1973, pp. 42-47, and May 8,
1973, pp. 79-83.

Baisho Mondai Kenkyukai, Nippon no Baisho: Sono Genjo to Mondaiten. Tokyo: Gaiko Johosha, 1959.

Cho, Yukio and Morita, Kiritaro. Yen no Shorai. Tokyo: Asahi Shimbun Sha, 1971.

Eguchi, Yujiro. "Betonaumu Fukko Enjo no Hoko," Ekonomisuto, June 19, 1974, pp. 75-79.

Hara, Kakuten, ed. Enjo no Jittai to Keizai Seisaku. Tokyo: Ajia Keizai Kenkyu Jo, 1969.

____. Gendai Ajia Keizai Ron. Tokyo: Keiso Shobo, 1971.

____. Kankoku Keizai no Kiseki. Tokyo: Nippon Kokusai Mondai Kenkyu Jo, 1970.

Honda, Kenkichi. Teikaihatsu Keizai Ron no Kozo. Tokyo: Shin Hyoron Sha, 1970.

Hotta, Yoshie. et al. Toron: Nippon no Naka no Ajia. Tokyo: Heibon Sha, 1973.

Imagawa, Ei-ichi and Matsuo, Hiroshi. Nikka Haiseki. Tokyo: Nippon Keizai Shimbun Sha, 1973.

Inoue, Ryuichiro. Kokusai Zaibatsu no Senryaku. Tokyo: Daiyamondo Sha, 1971.

Ishida, Masami. Atarashii Ajia Kaihatsu no Genjutsu. Tokyo: Daiyamondo Sha, 1970.

Itagaki, Yoichi and Yamamoto, Noboru. Namboku Mondai no Riron to Genjutsu. Tokyo: Nippon Kokusai Mondai Kenkyu Jo, 1969.

Kajima Heiwa Kenkyu Jo, ed. Taigai Keizai Kyoryoku Taikei, Vol. 1, Keizai Kyoryoku no Rinen to Hatten. Tokyo: Kajima Kenkyu Jo Shuppan Kai, 1973.

____. Taigai Keizai Kyoryoku Taikei, Vol. 2, Teikaihatsu Chiiki no Shomondai. Tokyo: Kajima Kenkyu Jo Shuppan Kai, 1973.

____. Taigai Keizai Kyoryoku Taikei, Vol. 3, Keizai Kyoryoku no Keitai. Tokyo: Kajima Kenkyu Jo Shuppan Kai, 1973.

____. Taigai Keizai Kyoryoku Taikei, Vol. 4, Tasukoku kan no Keizai Kyoryoku. Kajima Kenkyu Jo Shuppan Kai, 1974.

_____. Taigai Keizai Kyoryoku Taikei, Vol. 5, Nippon no Keizai Kyoryoku. Tokyo: Kajima Kenkyu Jo Shuppan Kai, 1973.

_____. Taigai Keizai Kyoryoku Taikei, Vol. 7, Ajia ni Taisuru Keizai Kyoryoku. Tokyo: Kajima Kenkyu Jo Shuppan Kai, 1974.

_____. Taigai Keizai Kyoryoku Taikei, Vol. 8, Ajia ni okeru Chiiki Kyoryoku. Tokyo: Kajima Shuppan Kai, 1973.

_____. Taigai Keizai Kyoryoku Taikei. Vol. 9, Chukinto, Afurika ni Taisuru Keizai Kyoryoku. Kajima Kenkyu Jo Shuppan Kai, 1973.

_____. Taigai Keizai Kyoryoku Taikei. Vol. 10, Chunanbei ni Taisuru Keizai Kyoryoku. Tokyo: Kajima Kenkyu Jo Shuppan Kai, 1973.

_____. Taigai Keizai Kyoryoku Taikei, Bekkan 1, Juyo Shiryo Shu. Tokyo: Kajima Kenkyu Jo Shuppan Kai, 1973.

_____. Taigai Keizai Kyoryoku Taikei, Bekkan 2, Keizai Kyoryoku Jitsumu, Keizai Kyoryoku Kankei Horei Kihon Bunsho Shu. Tokyo: Kajima Kenkyu Jo Shuppan kai, 1974.

Itagaki, Yoichi, ed. Namboku Mondai. Tokyo: Toyo Keizai Shimpo Sha, 1971.

Komai, Hiroshi. Taino Kindai Ka. Tokyo: Nippon Kokusai Mondai Kenkyu Jo. 1971.

Kanamori, Hisao. Keizai Taikoku "Nippon". Tokyo: Nippon Keizai Shimbun Sha, 1970.

Kasai, Akihiro. "Chugoku wa Naze Baisho o Toranakattaka," Chuo Koron, March 1973, pp. 93-101.

Kawata, Tadashi. Gendai Kokusai Keizai ron. Tokyo: Iwanami Shoten, 1971.

_____. "Sho Nippon Shugi" no Susume: Heiwa no Tame no Keizai Gaku. Tokyo: Daiyamondo Sha, 1972.

Kato, Hiroshi. Kokusaika Jidai no Kigyo to Seifu. Tokyo: Kogaku Sha, 1971.

Keizai Doyukai, ed. Gijitsu Kakushin to Keizai Shakai no Henbo. Tokyo: Kajima Kenkyu Jo Shuppan Kai, 1968.

Koizum, Akira and Aihara, Hikaru. Kokusai Keizai Ron Kogi. Tokyo:
Seirin Shoin Shinsha, 1972.

Kojima, Kiyoshi. Taiheiyo Keizaiken to Nippon. Tokyo: Kinimoto
Shobo, 1969.

Kokusai Kaihatsu Senta. Takokukan Enjo Kiko no Kenkyu. Tokyo:
Kokusai Kaihatsu Senta, 1972.

Kosho, Genji. Teikaihatsu Koku no Kaihatsu to Gijutsu Kyoryoku.
Tokyo: Ajia Keizai Kenkyu Jo, 1966.

Kurimoto, Hiroshi. Ajia no Keizai Seisho. Tokyo: 1969.

Matsumoto, Shigekazu and Ishida, Heiichiro. Taiwan no Keizai
Kaihatsu to Gaikoku Shihon. Tokyo: Ajia Keizai Kenkyu Jo, 1971.

Matsumoto, Shigekazu. Shogaikoku no Taiwan Enjo to Ni-chhu
Kankei. Tokyo: Ajia Keizai Kenkyu Jo, 1970.

Morita, Fumiyo. Sengo Nippon Shihon Shugi. To o: Aoki Shoten,
1972.

Morita, Kiriro. Namboku Mondai. Tokyo: Nihon Hyron Sha, 1967.

Nagasu, Kazuji. Nanshin suru Nippon Shihon Shugi. Tokyo: Mainichi
Shimbun Sha, 1971.

_____. Keizai Taikoku no Nanmon. Tokyo: Ushio Chuppan Sha, 1973.

_____. Sekai Keizai to Nippon: 70-nen Dai no Nippon. Tokyo: Asahi
Shimbun Sha, 1970.

Nakane, Chie. Tekio no Joken. Tokyo: Kodansha, 1972.

Nakayama, Sohei and Kasai, Akihiro. Zaikaijin no Ishiki Kakumei o
Motomeru. Chuo Koron, 1973, pp. 62-71.

Namiki, Yoshinobu. Kokusai Keizai Jidai no Nippon. Tokyo: Mainichi
Shimbun Sha, 1972.

Negishi, Tomijiro, ed. Ajia Shin Jidai no Kuniguni. Tokyo: Mainichi
Shimbun Sha, 1972.

Nawa, Taro. Tsusansho. Tokyo: Kyoikusha, 1974.

Nippon Keizai Shimbun Sha, <u>Nanboku Mondai Nyumon.</u> Tokyo: Nippon Keizai Shimbun Sha, 1971.

Nippon Sinku Tanku Kyokai, <u>Nippon no Genkai to Kanosei.</u> Tokyo: Nippon Noritsu Kyokai, 1973.

Nishi, Kazuo. <u>Keizai Kyoryoku.</u> Tokyo: Chuo Koron Sha, 1970.

Okita, Saburo. <u>Ekonomisuto no Yakuwari.</u> Tokyo: Nippon Keizai Shimbun Sha, 1973.

_____. <u>Teikaihatsu Koku no Boeki to Kaihatsu.</u> Tokyo: Nippon Keizai Shimbun Sha.

_____. "Tonan Ajia no Genjo Hokoku," <u>Kokusai Kaihatsu Janaru,</u> February 5, 1973, pp. 7-11.

Okita, Saburo and Kojima, Kiyoshi, eds. <u>Ajia Taiheiyo Kyoryoku eno Tenbo.</u> Tokyo: Nippon Kokusai Mondai Kenkyu Jo, 1971.

Onishi, Akira. <u>Teikaihatsu Koku to Nippon.</u> Tokyo: Nippon Kanzei Kyokai, 1969.

_____. <u>Kaihatsu Enjo.</u> Tokyo: Nippon Keizai Shimbun Sha, 1973.

Saito, Kazuo. "Nippon no Nogyo Kyoryoku no Atarashii Arikata," <u>Sekai Keizai Hyoron,</u> September 1973, 37-42.

Sankei Shimbun Ajia Shuzai Han. <u>Rinjin Tachi no Sugao: Baisho to Enjo no Tanima de.</u> Tokyo: Sankei Shimbun Sha Shuppan Kyoku, 1971.

Seidensticker, Edward et al. <u>Han-nichi Kanjo.</u> Tokyo: Nishin Hodo, 1973.

Shibata, Hiroshi, <u>Kokusai Keizai Seisaku no Riron.</u> Tokyo: Toyo Keizai Shimpo.

Shinohara, Miyohei. <u>Keizai Seicho.</u> Tokyo: Tsukuma Shobo, 1970.

Shishido, Toshio. <u>Tonan Ajia Enjo o Kangaeru.</u> Tokyo: Toyo Keizai Shimpo Sha, 1973.

Shimomura, Osamu. <u>Keizai Taikoku Nippon no Sentaku.</u> Tokyo: Toyo Keizai Shimpo Sha, 1971.

Tai Kuo Hui, <u>Nippon Jin Tono Taiwa.</u> Tokyo: Shakai Shiso Sha, 1970.

Takahashi, Osamu. Minikui Nippon Jin. Tokyo: Hara Shobo, 1970.

Takada, Tsutomu. Mitsui Bussan no Sekai Senryaku. Tokyo: Gakushu Kenkyu Sha, 1969.

Toba, Kin-ichiro. Futatsu no Kao no Nippon Jin. Tokyo: Chuo Koron Sha, 1973.

Tobata, Seiichi and Yano, Seiya, eds. Ajia no Keizai Seicho. Tokyo: Toyo Keizai Shinpo Sha, 1970.

Tonan Ajia Chosa Kai, Tonan Ajia Yoran. Tokyo: Jiji Press, 1969.

Uchida, Tadao. "Sekiyu Kiki wa Nippon Keizai Kaizo no Koki." Ekonomisuto, December 4, 1973, pp. 28-33.

Yamamoto, Noboru and Itagaki, Yo-ichi, eds. Namboku Mondai no Riron to Genjutsu. Tokyo: Nippon Kokusai Mondai Kenkyu Jo, 1969.

Yamashita, Maso and Aki, Koichi. Tonan Ajia no Keizai. Tokyo: Jiji Press, 1969.

Yamazaki, Kiyoshi. "Nippon Kigyo Takokuseki-ka eno Tembo," Ekonomisuto, October 1972.

Yomiyuri Shimbun Sha, Denaose Keizai Taikoku. Tokyo: Daiyamondo Sha, 1972.

Yoshizawa, Seijiro. Indo-Himaraya Shokoku. Tokyo: Kajima Heiwa Kenkyu Jo, 1969.

Yukizawa, Kenzo. "Ajia ni okeru Nippon no Sentaku," Ekonomisuto, May 1, 197 , pp. 35-40.

____. Nippon Keizai to Ajia. Tokyo: Asahi Shimbun Sha, 1970.

Watanabe, Takeshi, Ajia Kaigin Sosai Nikki. Tokyo: Nippon Keizai Shimbun Sha, 1973.

In Other Languages

Adelman, Irma and Morris, Cynthia. Society, Politics, and Economic Development: A Quantitative Approach. Baltimore: Johns Hopkins University Press, 1967.

166

Adelman, Irma. Theories of Economic Growth and Development. Stanford: Stanford University Press, 1961.

Appelbaum, Richard P. Theories of Social Change. Chicago: Markham Publishing Company, 1970.

Asher, Robert and Eckaus, R.S. (eds.) Development of the Emerging Countries An Agenda for Research. Washington D.C.: Brookings Institution, 1962.

Asher, Robert E. "Economic Co-operation under UN Auspices," International Organization. (Summer, 1958). Vol. 12, no. 3, pp. 288-302.

_____. "Multilateral versus Bilateral Aid: an Old Controversy Revisited," International Organization. (Autumn 1962). Vol. 16, no. 4, pp. 697-719.

Asher, Robert E., Kotschning, Walter M. and Brown, William (eds.) The United Nations and Economic and Social Cooperation, Washington D.C.: Brookings Institution, 1957.

Badgley, John. Asian Development: Problems and Prognosis. New York: Free Press, 1971.

Basch, Antonin. "International Bank for Reconstruction and Development," International Conciliation. November, 1949.

Bennett, John W., Hasegawa, Sukehiro and Levine, Solomon B. "Japan; Environment (December 1973), pp. 6-13.

Black, Eugene R. Alternative in Southeast Asia, New York: Praeger, 1969.

Bornsteim, Morris (ed.) Comparative Economic System. Homewood: Richard Irwin, 1965.

Boserup, Ester and Sachs, Ignacy (eds.) Aide exterieure aux pays recement independants: Problems et orientations. Le aye: Mouton, 1971.

Brown, Lester R. Seeds of Change. New York: Praeger, 1972.

Chenery, Hollis B. (ed.) Studies in Development Planning. Cambridge, Mass.: Harvard University Press, 1971.

_____. and Taylor, L. "Development Patterns: Among Countries and Over Time," Review of Economics and Statistics. (November, 1968.)

Demerath, Nicholas J. "Can India Reduce its Birth Rate? A Question of Modernization and Governmental Capacity," Journal of Social Issues. Vol XXIII, No. 4, 1967.

Dimock, Marshall. A Philosophy of Administration. New York: Harper and Row, 1965.

Fei, J. C. and Ranis, G. Development of the Labor Surplus Economy: Theory and Policy. Homewood: Irwin, 1964.

Feis, Herbert. Foreign Aid and Foreign Policy. New York: St. Martin's Press, 1964.

Feuer, G. "Une creation originale des Nations Unies en matier d'assistance technique: les service internationale d'administrateurs," Annuaire Francaise de Droit International, 1959, pp. 522-542.

Frank, Charles R. "Optimal Terms of Foreign Assistance," Journal of Political Economy. (September-October, 1970), pp. 1107-1114.

Friedmann, Wolfgang G., Kalmanoff, George, and Meagher, Robert. International Financial Aid. New York: Columbia University Press, 1966.

Friedmann, Wolfgang G. and Beguin, Jean-Pierre. Joint International Business Ventures in Developing Countries: Studies and Analysis of Recent Trends. New York: Columbia University Press, 1971.

Gardner, Richard and Millikan, Max F. The Global Partnership. New York: Praeger, 1968.

Goldscheider, Calvin. Population, Modernization and Social Structure. Boston: Little, Brown and Co., 1971.

Goulet, Denis. The Cruel Choice: a New Concept in the Theory of Development. New York: Atheneum, 1973.

Halliday, Jon and McCormack, Gavan. Japanese Imperialism Today. London: Penguin Books, 1973.

168

Haas, Ernst. Beyond the Nation-State: Functionalism and International Organization. Stanford: Stanford University Press, 1964.

Hayter, Teresa. Aid as Imperialism. Middlesex, England: Penguin, 1971.

Hawthorne, Edward. The Transfer of Technology. Paris: OECD, 1971.

Hedberg, Hakan H. The Japanese Challenge. Translated by Yasushi Sekiguchi. Tokyo: Asahi Shimbun, 1970.

Hirschman, Albert O. The Strategy of Economic Development. New Haven: Yale University Press, 1959.

____. Foreign Aid-A Critique and Proposal. Princeton: Princeton University Press, 1968.

Hicks, George and McNicoll, Georffrey. Trade and Growth in the Philippines An Open Dual Economy. Ithaca: Cornell University Press, 1971.

Hoadley, J. Stephen and Hasegawa, Sukehiro. "Sino-Japanese Relations: 1950-1970: An Application of the Linkage Model of International Relations," International Studies Quarterly. (June 1971), pp. 131-157.

Hollerman, Leon. Japan's Dependence on the World Economy: The Approach Toward Economic Liberalization. Princeton: Princeton University Press, 1967.

Horowitz, Irving Louis. The Worlds of Development. New York: Oxford University Press, 1972.

Huddle, Franklin P. The Mekong: Opportunities and Problems of Regionalism. Prepared for the Subcommittee on National Security Policy and Scientific Developments of the Committee on Foreign Affairs, U. S. House of Representatives. (May 1972).

Huntington, Samuel P. "Foreign Aid: For What and For Whom," Development Today. eds. Robert E. Hunter and John E. Rielly. New York: Praeger, 1972.

Ike, Nobutaka. Japanese Politics. New York: Alfred Knoph, 1973.

Jacoby, N. H. An Evaluation of US Economic Aid to Free China: 1951-1965. Washington, D. C.: Aid for International Development, 1966.

Johnson, Harry G. Economic Policies Toward Less Developed Countries. New York: Praeger, 1967.

Johnson, Walter L. and Kamerschen, David R. Reading in Economic Development. Cincinnati: Southwesterns Publishing Co., 1972.

Kindleberger, Charles P. Economic Development. New York: McGraw-Hill, 1965.

_____. International Economics. Chicago: Irwin, 1963.

_____. American Business Abroad. New Haven. Yale University Press, 1969.

Kaplan, Jacob J. The Challenge of Foreign Aid. New York: Praeger, 1967.

Little, L. M. D. and Clifford, J. M. International Aid. Chicago: Aldine, 1965.

Lockwood, William W. The State and Economic Enterprise in Japan. Princeton: Princeton University Press, 1965.

Langdon, F. C. Japan's Foreign Policy. Vancouver: University of British Columbia Press, 1973.

Louffi, M. F. The Net Cost of Japanese Foreign Aid. New York: Praeger, 1973.

Mason, Edward S. Foreign Aid and Foreign Policy. New York: Harper and Row, 1964.

_____. and Asher, Robert E. The World Bank Since Bretton Woods. Washington, D. C.: Brookings Institution, 1973.

Mason, Hal. The Transfer of Technology and the Factor Proportions Problem: The Philippines and Mexico. New York: UNITAR, 1971.

Mikesell, Raymond. The Economics of Foreign Aid. Chicago: Aldine, 1968.

_____. U. S. Private and Government Investment Abroad. Eugene, Oregon: University of Oregon Books, 1962.

Montgomery, Joh D. The Politics of Foreign Aid. Chicago: Aldine, 1968.

170

_____. Foreign Aid in International Politics. Englewood-Cliffs, N. J.: Prentice-Hall, 1967.

Morgan, Robert. "Transfer of Technology," Douglas A. Chalmer, ed. Changing Latin America. August 1972. Proceeding of Academy of Political Science.

Morgenthau, Hans. "A Political Theory of Foreign Aid," American Political Science Review. June 1962, pp. 4-5-406.

Myint, H. Southeast Asia's Economy: Development Policies in the 1970's. New York: Praeger, 1972.

Myrdal, Gunnar. Asian Drama. New York: Vintage Books, 1968.

_____. The Challenge of World Poverty. New York: Vintage Books, 1970.

Nakamura, Hajime. Ways of Thinking of Eastern Peoples: India, China, Tibet, Japan. Honolulu: East-West Center Press, 1964.

Nakane, Chie. Japanese Society. Berkeley: University of California Press, 1970.

Ohlin, Goran. Foreign Aid Politices Reconsidered. Paris: OECD, 1966.

Okita, Saburo. Causes and Problems of Rapid Growth in Post-war Japan and Their Implication for Newly Developing Countries. Tokyo: Japan Economic Research Center, 1967.

_____. "Natural Resources Dependency and Japanese Foreign Policy," Foreign Affairs. vol. 52 no. 4, July 1974, pp. 714-24.

O'leary, Michael K. The Politics of American Foreign Aid. New York: Atherton Press, 1967.

Olson, Lawrence. Japan in Postwar Asia. New York: Praeger, 1970.

Owens, Edgar and Shaw, Robert. Development Reconsidered. Lexington Mass.: Lexington Books, 1972.

Ozaki, Robert S. "Japan's Role in Asian Economic Development," Asian Survey, April 1967, pp. 237-44.

Pearson, Lester B. et. al. Partners in Development. New York: Praeger, 1969.

Pincus, John. Economic Aid and International Cost Sharing. Baltimore: Johns Hopkins Press, 1965.

Reischauer, Edwin O. The United States and Japan. New York: Viking Press, 1965.

Schmidt, Wilson E. "The Economics of Charity: Loans versus Grants," Journal of Political Economy, August 1964, pp. 387-95.

Shibuya, Yukio and Yamashita, Shoichi. Foreign Aid and Economic Growth of Developing Asian Countries. Tokyo: Institute of Developing Economies, 1968.

Thorp, Williard L. The Reality of Foreign Aid. New York: Praeger, 1971.

Tickner, Fred. Technical Cooperation. New York: Praeger, 1965.

Walters, Robert S. Americans and Soviet Aid. Pittsburgh: University of Pittsburgh Press, 1970.

Ward, Robert. Japan's Political System. Englewood Cliffs: Prentice-Hall, 1967.

White, John. Japanese Aid. London: Overseas Development Institute, 1964.

Wolf, Charles. Foreign Aid: Theory and Practice in Southern Asia. Princeton: Princeton University Press, 1960.

SUKEHIRO HASEGAWA is Area Officer for Burma and Hong Kong in the Regional Bureau for Asia and the Far East, United Nations Development Programme (UNDP). Since he joined UNDP in 1969, he acted as Project Officer in the Bureau for Programming and Operations and Area Officer for Pakistan and the Philippines in the Regional Bureau.

Dr. Hasegawa has published in the area of political economy and human environment. His articles have appeared in International Studies Quarterly and Environment.

Dr. Hasegawa holds an A. B. from the University of Michigan, MAPA from the Graduate School of Public Administration, ICU, Tokyo, and Ph. D. from Washington University, St. Louis.

RELATED TITLES
Published by
Praeger Special Studies

THE NET COST OF JAPANESE FOREIGN AID
                    Martha F. Loutfi

JAPANESE PRIVATE ECONOMIC DIPLOMACY: An
Analysis of Business-Government Linkages
                    William R. Bryant

JAPANESE INVESTMENT IN THE UNITED STATES:
With a Case Study of the Hawaiian Experience
                    H. Robert Heller
                    Emily E Heller

CHINESE AND SOVIET AID TO AFRICA
                    edited by
                    Warren Weinstein

SOVIET AND CHINESE INFLUENCE IN THE THIRD
WORLD
                    edited by
                    Alvin Z. Rubinstein

AID AND DEVELOPMENT: A Handbook for Small
Doners
                    Marian Radetzki